C000090597

THE A-Z OF CURIOUS

NOTTINGHAMSHIRE

To Howard
best wishes tu
a good fan

A. Evp.

THE A-Z OF CURIOUS

NOTTINGHAMSHIRE

STRANGE STORIES OF MYSTERIES, CRIMES AND ECCENTRICS

FRANK E. EARP

The
History
Press

'AY-UP MI DUCK'

*A traditional Nottinghamshire greeting, thought to derive from the
Old Norse* Se upp, *meaning to 'look out' or 'watch out'.
Dialect: 'mi' – 'my' and the Anglo-Saxon Duka, literally 'Duke'.*

First published 2014

The History Press
The Mill, Brimscombe Port
Stroud, Gloucestershire, GL5 2QG
www.thehistorypress.co.uk

© Frank E. Earp, 2014

The right of Frank E. Earp to be identified as the Author
of this work has been asserted in accordance with the
Copyright, Designs and Patents Act 1988.

All rights reserved. No part of this book may be reprinted
or reproduced or utilised in any form or by any electronic,
mechanical or other means, now known or hereafter invented,
including photocopying and recording, or in any information
storage or retrieval system, without the permission in writing
from the Publishers.

British Library Cataloguing in Publication Data.
A catalogue record for this book is available from the British Library.

ISBN 978 0 7509 5442 6

Typesetting and origination by The History Press
Printed in Great Britain

Contents

Acknowledgements

I HAVE BEEN studying the folklore and history of Nottinghamshire for over forty years now, and there are many people who I must thank for their help and advice. All of these people have helped contribute to my accumulated knowledge which has led to me to writing this book. You know who you are, so thank you, all of you!

Specifically, thanks go to Peter Hannah, who back in the early days was my partner in research. My thanks go to the late Paul Nix, whose expertise, particularly in the subject of Nottingham's caves, has constantly inspired me, and to Dr Robert Morrell, an early pioneer in the history and folklore of Nottinghamshire.

I would like to thank my youngest son Joseph 'Joe' Earp, who is following in his father's footsteps; John Howorth, Editor of the *Topper* newspaper, for allowing me to publish my weekly articles in the paper; and Robert 'Bob' Trubshaw for his help and inspiration and providing his contribution to this work.

Finally, my thanks go to the good citizens of Nottinghamshire, past and present, for making the county such a 'curious' place.

Introduction

THE DICTIONARY DEFINES the word curiosity as the desire to know about something. It is also used to refer to that about which the desire for knowledge is sought. Curiosity may have killed the cat, but it is one of the things that make us human. It is curiosity that has brought society knowledge.

So, what 'curiosities' does the County of Nottinghamshire have? 'Tigguacobauc', now there is a curious word, even if you understand its meaning. But this may have been the first recorded name for the settlement that is now the City of Nottingham.

Nottingham has two infamous curiosities: its caves and its alleged most famous son, 'Robin Hood'. There are around 500 artificial caves under the city, each of which is a curiosity in its own right. There have been many things written about Robin, good, bad and indifferent. Rather than contribute something more to the pot, I have chosen instead to provide a list of places and objects which bear his name.

As the reader will find out, there is more to Nottingham and its county than Robin Hood and the caves. I have always been curious to know how it all began, what was on Castle Rock, BC (Before the Castle)?

Excellent examples are the 'curiosities' contained within these pages inlcude the county's three 'Old Stones', natural geological features which for tens of thousands of years have witnessed the passage of time and human history.

Nottinghamshire had and probably still does have its eccentrics, people like Benjamin Mayo, the 'Old General', Frank Robinson, 'The Xylophone Man' and Kitty Hudson, the girl who ate pins.

The county has seen its share of violence and crime, like the murder of Elizabeth Sheppherd and highwaymen like 'Swift Nick' and 'Sawly Tom'.

They say that there are more ghosts per square mile in Britain than any other country in the world. Nottingham certainly has its fair share of ghost and hauntings, and I have included six of the least-known supernatural tales.

It was curiosity that brought the American writer Washington Irvin to Nottinghamshire and led him to spend Yule (Christmas) 1824 in the heart of Sherwood Forest. It was at Newstead Abbey that he witnessed many of the curious customs of the season.

Running like a thread through this book is an ancient highway now known as 'Mansfield Road'. It is curious how it relates to and connects many of the people and places mentioned within these pages.

I hope that this introduction has made the reader curious enough to read on!

Frank E. Earp, 2014

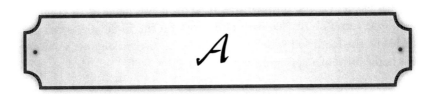

A

⚜ ANCIENT NOTTINGHAM

Prehistoric Earthworks, Ancient Mounds and a Roman Tower

Soon after the Norman Conquest of 1066, a castle was built on the top of the massive sandstone promontory Castle Rock, which juts out from the hills like a great stone monolith. On the south side the cliff face rises 130ft (38m) from the road. Over the millennium, at all levels, it has become full of caves and has taken on the appearance of a great Swiss cheese. This may be considered one of the finest views the city has to offer.

It is inconceivable that this truly impressive site had not been used before. What did the Normans find here when they came to build the castle? Certainly they found many caves excavated into the cliff face. We may believe that this was Asser's 'Tigguacobauc' – 'cavy house' – the earliest recorded name for a settlement in the Nottingham area.

The Normans would also have found that someone had cutoff the promontory from the hill on the north and east side with a massive ditch – in places cut into the bedrock over 30ft deep. That the ditch was already old when the Normans arrived is attested to by the fact that it was being used as a Saxon boundary. There is no evidence to suggest that the Saxons had settled around this site. It is generally agreed that the settlement of 'Snottingham', which gave the city its name, was somewhere in the area of the Lace Market, around half a mile to the east. It is unlikely then, that the Saxons would have gone to the considerable effort of constructing such a massive earthwork and the likelihood is that it was prehistoric.

The ditch starts on the eastern side, at the foot of Castle Rock, and follows the line of Castle Road up the hill to the castle gates. This section was utilised by the Normans as a dry moat – the eastern outer defences of the castle. It was later to become a medieval sunken road known as 'The Hollows'. At a point almost opposite the statue of Robin Hood, another old road – Hounds Gate – joins Castle Road on its right-hand side. Here, in 1779, workmen excavating to a depth of 14ft discovered what they described as 'a solid cart road'.

From this point the course of the ditch takes a north-westerly turn along the line of the road known as Standard Hill. In places the road surface is built directly over the line of the ditch. Building on the south side of Standard Hill and Postern Street has always proven problematic. In 1807, it was decided to build a new church – St James's – on Standard Hill. Work on the foundations was greatly impeded by the loose soil which was infilling the ancient ditch. A solution was found in the form of a 'springing arch' bridging the ditch.

The eastern face of the mighty Castle Rock. (Joe Earp, 2013, Nottingham Hidden History Team)

When work started on the new extensions to the General Hospital, evidence of this massive ditch was once again exposed. Foundations for the Round Ward – now The Round House – were particularly troublesome. The ditch here was found to be between 50ft and 60ft wide and 33ft deep. To make matters worse, a second parallel ditch – 13ft wide and 17ft deep – was found a few feet to the north.

The ditch continues its course along Postern Street to its junction with Park Row. Here, it takes a 90 degree turn to the left and continues for several yards before terminating just before the gates of the old General Hospital. Here on its southern side the ditch partly enclosed an open field said to be an 'ancient camp'.

The Derry Mount

Mystery surrounds the Derry Mount and its place in history. There appears to be no references to the mount earlier than the seventeenth century, nor does it appear on any early maps. In 1904, the Thoroton Society published an old plan of the castle superimposed on a modern street plan. The mount – which is described as being 'now levelled' – is marked between Mount Street and Park Row. This would place it to the rear of the modern buildings on the north side of Postern Street, close to its junction with Park Row.

At the outbreak of the Civil War in 1642, King Charles I was at the castle to rally support for his cause. He began by raising his flag or royal standard above the castle ramparts, but this did not produce the desired effect. On 22 August 1642, with great ceremony, the King and his retinue proceeded to a spot 'just north of the castle gateway', and once again the standard was raised. The rest, as they say, is history.

One account of this momentous event names the site as the 'Derry Mount'. However, another account simple describes it as, 'a flat, round spot on the top of a rocky knoll'. For several years, a wooden post marked the exact spot, until the site changed ownership and it was removed. The location became known as Standard Hill and as the green fields gave way to buildings the site was marked by a plaque commemorating the event.

Was the Derry Mount a prehistoric mound? It is interesting to note that as a place name, Derry is derived from an ancient Gaelic word meaning (sacred) 'oak grove' – as with Londonderry or simply Derry in Ireland.

The Deity Mound

A second artificial mound, the Deity Mound, also claims to be the spot where the King raised his standard. J. Holland Walker states: 'On the site where the old children's hospital stands was a mysterious mound which was called Deity Mount [*sic*], and the history of which is obscure. It seems to have been prehistoric in origin, and was not cleared away till the Seventeenth Century.' The Thoroton map identifies it as the 'standard raising site' and locates it around the centre of the 'ancient camp', mentioned above.

Caesar's Tower

All of the sites looked at so far have been outside the precincts of the medieval castle. It is inconceivable that this spectacular site remained vacant until the eleventh century. Is there evidence of occupation before this date? A number of Victorian historians mention a reference to Caesar's Tower in 'old documents', relating to 'The Treaty of Nottingham'.

The documents tell how, in 867, the Viking army led by the Dane Ivor Ragnarsson – Ivor the Boneless – captured Nottingham in an incursion south from their base in York. The Vikings are said to have taken up residence in 'a strong tower' – the remains of a Roman fort – on the summit of Castle Rock.

A year later, the Saxons, led by Ethelred of Wessex and his brother Alfred the Great, besieged Ivor's forces. The Vikings refused to surrender and, such was the strength of their fortifications, the Saxons were force to make a treaty. The Treaty of Nottingham allowed Ivor to remain in Nottingham in return for making no further raids into the Kingdom of Mercia. A year later, the treaty was broken and the Vikings withdrew back to York.

The Treaty of Nottingham is certainly a well-documented historic event. But what of the part relating to Caesar's Tower? If this is to be believed, it opens a whole new aspect to Nottingham's history. Modern historians have tended to largely dismiss this reference as fanciful partly on the grounds that Roman forts do not feature what might be determined as a strong tower. However, there is another kind of Roman building which adequately fits, not only the description but also the location. Could it be that Caesar's Tower was the remains of a Roman signal station?

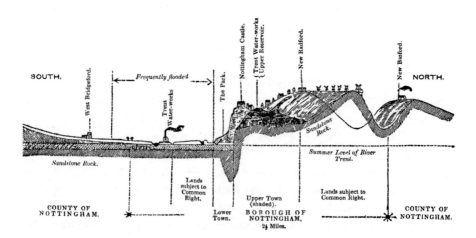

A cut-away view of Nottingham's ridge-line from the east. (Courtesy of the Paul Nix Collection)

These stations consisted of towers of various sizes, fortified by a surrounding wall or bank and ditch. Their purpose was to relay messages using a highly effective telegraph system of flags by day and beacon firers by night. Signal stations are found all over the Empire and there are many examples in Britain. In the third century AD Roman Britain came under the threat of invasion from European Germanic tribes – the Saxons and others. To counter this threat, a series of signal stations were built along the Yorkshire coast. The example illustrated is from Filey. A tower built on Castle Rock, with its commanding views, would have been ideally placed to guard against incursions along the tidal River Trent and quickly summon help from the Roman garrison in Leicester.

❧ BAGGULEY (POSTMAN) AND JOHN MARTYN: ❧ ACCIDENTAL DEATH OR MANSLAUGHTER?

John Martyn was the well-known landlord of Ye Lether Bottell public house, which once stood at the corner of Mansfield Road and Forest Lane, formerly Bottle Lane. The inn had been the home and source of income for the Martyn family for several generations.

Outside the inn, close to the centre of the main road, stood an ancient guide stone, then in use as a mounting block. One of Martyn's ancestors, also a John, had carved an inscription in doggerel verse on the Mansfield side of the stone: 'John Martyn Stone I am / shows ye great road to Nottingham. 1621.'

Although there was a regular mail coach between Nottingham and Leeds, the post for Mansfield was still delivered on foot by a postman. In the 1790s, the round was the responsibility of veteran letter carrier, 69-year-old John Bagguley. Bagguley would walk from Nottingham to Mansfield carrying the post. On arrival at his destination he would ring a hand bell in the streets to signify his presence. The good folk of the town would gather about him to see if there was a letter for them or to hand him mail that they wished delivered to Nottingham.

The winter of 1796/7 had been hard, and one morning in late February 1797 when Bagguley set out, the snow lay thick on the ground. By the time he reached Seven Mile House, the snow had again begun to fall. On reaching The Hutt, Bagguley was advised to wait until the weather had cleared or turn back. However, he insisted on continuing with his delivery.

As he left the warmth and safety of The Hutt, who can say what was going through the mind of John Bagguley? The greater part of his journey still lay ahead. How long it took him to reach the Lether Bottel we cannot say, but we know that by the time he reached the familiar landmark, the great guide stone was almost covered in snow.

Bagguley was now exhausted and, summoning what was left of his strength, he knocked on the inn door and demanded entry 'in the King's name!' It is said that from an upstairs window, Martyn called back that he should 'go to hell!' Bagguley struggled on to a spot around where Mansfield F.C. now stands, before finally collapsing. His frozen corpse was later found, still clutching the mail bag. John Bagguley was buried with much acclaim in Mansfield Churchyard on 1 March 1797.

Bagguley's death shocked the town and Martyn was summoned to court to answer for his part. However, there was little evidence to convict him of manslaughter and all that the magistrates could do was to deprive the Martyn family of their living by ordering that the inn be closed and that the house never again be granted a licence. At this point in the story, Martyn disappears into the pages of history. In a strange twist, the great guide stone also disappeared from its place in the road. The inn became a private house and passed through many hands. There the story might have ended. When the house was finally demolished, the old stone was found lying in its cellar. The stone proved too large to pass through the cellar's hatch and was ignominiously broken up.

⁂ BOGGART (THE) ⁂

A Close Encounter of the 'Furred' Kind
This is the story of my encounter with a boggart, although I did not know it as such at the time. I first published this story in the journal of the Northern Earth Mysteries Group, in early 1981. It was picked up by the ufologist Jenny Randels and appeared in the part-work magazine *The Unexplained* in 1983. In 1989, Paul Devereux used it in support of his theory on the UFO phenomenon, in his book *Earth Lights*. From then on it quickly passed into modern folklore and now appears on several websites.

In the mid-1960s, Britain was in the grip of UFO fever. Up and down the country there were reports of lights in of sky and other unidentified objects. For several weeks the media reported strange goings-on in the town of Warminster, in Wiltshire. Nottingham too had its fair share of UFO activity. This was a fascination to a boy in his early teens and, together with a group of around ten school friends, we started a UFO club. Well, at least it kept us out of mischief – but it lead to many a strange adventure. The adventure related here happened with two of my fellow club members – whom I will call W and M.

On a fine autumn afternoon my friend W and I walked the mile or so up Chalbury Road to meet with fellow club member M. It was our intention to carry out what is known as a sky watch – looking for U.F.Os. From M's house, the three of us crossed Woodyard Lane to walk along the north bank of the disused Wollaton canal to the site of the Wollaton Colliery. Here, the old slag heaps line the Canal bank and we thought it would be a good vantage point for our activity.

We spent the next couple of hours scaling and sliding down the heaps and swinging out over the canal on a rope tied to the branch of a tree – always with an eye on the sky. At about four o'clock, as daylight gave way to twilight, we decided – as we had seen no 'flying saucers' – to head back to M's house and perhaps play some records.

At this site, the canal opens into a wide oval basin – a former passing place for the coal barges. Although the canal had been drained, the old bed was still marshy with a small channel of water running down the centre. As we crossed the basin to the opposite south bank, we were aware of a slight ground mist starting to rise within the basin.

Climbing up the wall and bank onto the towpath, we stood watching the mist as it began to thicken. As we watched, a cloud of mist – doughnut shaped, around the size of a fairground dodgem car – formed and rose above the bed to the height of around 4ft. The remaining body of mist, which now covered most of the basin, stayed within inches of the ground.

The cloud began to sparkle with a myriad of tiny pearl-coloured lights which blinked on and off with an incandescent glow. At this point I suggested this was the natural phenomenon known as 'corpse candles' or 'will o' the wisp' – the spontaneous combustion of methane gas.

Suddenly, the cloud began to slowly move towards the bank and two balls of light – the size of watermelons and around 2ft and 3ft apart – formed at its centre. In a controlled way, the cloud came to a halt on the towpath around 30ft away.

All around, afternoon was giving way to evening. In the growing darkness the spheres became more obvious, seeming to bob up and down like corks on water. No malevolence appeared to emanate from the cloud, just curiosity. It seemed that we, as observers, where in turn being observed. However, discretion got the better of valour and turning in unison we walked away.

After a few paces curiosity got the better of us and we stopped to look back. To our horror, the cloud had followed us and was now just 20ft away. Panic now set in and we retreated, this time at a jogging pace.

The canal now took a gentle turn and then a straight course to a point where Old Coach Road once crossed via a stone bridge. The bridge had long since disappeared and the road was now carried over the canal on a high bank, which the towpath climbed over on either side.

I had the sudden feeling that the 'thing' would not follow us across the road and voiced this fact to my friends. Frequent glances over our shoulders told us that the cloud was keeping pace behind, in fact it was gaining with every step.

Reaching the bank, we turned to see our pursuer was now just a few feet behind us. Seconds later, we mounted the bank and found ourselves looking down on the cloud, which had moved to the foot of the bank.

It seemed that the cloud would not follow us further. With relief, we crossed the road and descended onto the path. Now, with the bank between us, we felt safe to stand and look back. For a few seconds the road above was clear and then slowly the cloud came into view. Now hovering over the road at the top of the bank, 'it' was looking down at us!

We took off in full retreat, running in terror, the cloud still gliding effortlessly behind. At the pace we were travelling, it was not long before we reached Wood Yard Lane and the end of this part of the canal.

Here we turned to face our pursuer – now only 6ft away – safe in the knowledge that just across the lane was M's house. With me in the middle, we stood in silence, like gunfighters waiting for the next move. I broke the spell by taking a step forward and saying, 'If you are a friend come forward'.

A few seconds' silence followed as I paused for a response. With my eyes fixed on the swaying orbs I began to say, 'If you are an enemy –' My words were cut short as B tapped me on the shoulder and said in my ear, 'When I say run, run!' My eyes followed his pointing finger to the hedge on my left.

The boggart on the canal path. (Author's Illustration)

There, only feet in front of M, silhouetted by the light from the orbs, was the black shape of a hairy figure. Around 6ft tall, its head appeared to be directly on its shoulders, whilst its arms, which were very long, tapered to a single finger. Each of these fingers curved inward around a glowing red rod the size of a pencil. The legs seemed to disappear from around the mid-calf and something of the mist from the cloud swirled around where the feet should have been.

I had absorbed all of this information in seconds, for in an instant B had shouted 'Run!' and like an Olympic athlete taken off. I followed with the same turn of speed, leaving M alone, calling out, 'Can you see it lads? Can you see it?'

M must have quickly realised he was alone and soon caught us up. The other two began to blurt out their experience. I silenced them, saying that we should independently draw what we had seen. It turned out that the three of us drew identical pictures of the cloud, whilst B and I drew almost identical pictures of the figure. Because his attention had been entirely on the cloud, M hadn't seen the figure.

Years later I was to discover that our encounter had not been with some alien being. The hairy creature fitted the classic description of a class of fairy known as a boggart.

❧ BOOTY (RAYMOND CHARLES), 'THE FLYING BOOT' ❧

No one can have failed to have noticed the sudden rise in popularity of cycling in all its forms, as both a sport and leisure activity. It cannot be a coincidence that this rise began shortly after Bradley Wiggins' stunning win of the 2012 Tour de France. But, as they say, for cycling in Britain 'the best was yet to come!'

The 2012 Olympics and Paralympics saw the greatest ever success for Team Great Britain. Who can forget Sir Christopher (Chris) Hoy's dominance in the Velodrome? The names of the medal winners, both male and female, have rightly passed into history and their golden legacy is to be treasured.

In July 2013 – the centenary year of the Tour de France – another British cyclist, Chris Froome, repeated Wiggins' success and won the coveted yellow jersey.

In all sports the success of current athletes can only be built upon the generations who have gone before. For cycling, there is one man's name that should be written large across the page: the Nottingham-born Raymond (Ray) Charles Booty, aka 'The Flying Boot'. Sadly, Ray died on 25 August 2012. Given current events it seems an appropriate time to bring his story to a wider audience.

It is said that Ray achieved for road cycling what Sir Roger Bannister did for track-running – as Bannister broke the 4-minute mile record – Ray broke the 100 miles in 4 hours record.

Ray was a road cyclist who began competing in events for the Army Cycling Union during his time in the army and later for Ericsson's Wheelers Club.

Ray proved himself a born road cyclist and endurance rider. He held The Season Long – Best All-Rounder title three times between 1953 and 1957, given for average speeds of 50mph over 100 miles.

In 1954 Ray won the Manx International Road Race and in 1958 a 'Gold Medal' in the British and Commonwealth Games' Road Race in Cardiff. However, Ray's best achievements came in 'time trials' and endurance.

Between 1954 and 1958, Ray competed in the 12 Hours Championship – distance covered in 12 hours. Ray won the Championship every year and twice set the record – 1956 = 265.66 miles and 1958 = 266 miles.

Ray competed in the 100 miles National Championship between 1954 and 1959 and again was Champion for the whole period. He first set the record in 1955 with a time of 4 hours 4 minutes 30 seconds, breaking this in 1956 with a time of 4 hours 1 minute 52 seconds.

On a blazing hot August Bank Holiday Monday – 6 August 1956 – Ray entered the Bath Road event. This was a time trial, out and back over a distance of 100 miles. The course was from Reading through Theale, Pangbourne, Wallingford, Shillingford and Abingdon, returning to Reading via the A4. He had already cycled from Nottingham the day before to take part in the event. The Flying Boot completed the course in an amazing time of 3 hours 58 minutes 28 seconds, beating the future professional rider Stan Brittain by 12 minutes.

With the Bath Road event, Ray had broken the elusive 4-hour barrier. Modern cycling athletes ride purpose-built light-weight cycles – Ray achieved his records riding a Raleigh bicycle with an 84in fixed gear.

On 3 September the same year, The Flying Boot had his chance to beat his 4-hour record. This time he was competing under Road Record Association Rules. This is a straight-out 100-mile trial, which allows competitors to take advantage of tail winds and gradient drop. Ray had also changed his cycle for a machine with Sturmly Archer hub gears. Ray completed the course in a time of 3 hours 28 minutes 40 seconds – a record which was to stand for thirty-four years until it was beaten by Ian Cammish.

The next time you peddle down the road on your bike, think of the achievements of Raymond Charles Booty, The Flying Boot!

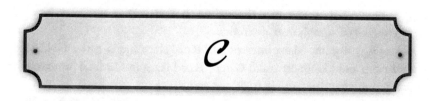

⚜ CENTRE STONE (THE): WHERE NELL GWYN ⚜ DROPPED HER LAST HANDKERCHIEF'

On the northern edge of Bestwood Park – once a part of Sherwood Forest – is the site of Bestwood Colliery. Its old engine house still stands as a mute testament to this once thriving pit. Known locally as the miner's path, the course of an old railway siding leads in a straight line from the colliery into the wooded slopes of the Park. Where the old line terminates at the foot of a steep slope, a modern path climbs further into the park. By the side of this path is an unremarkable ashlar (worked stone) known as the 'Centre Stone'.

The stone is roughly 2ft by 1ft and protrudes from the ground to around 2ft – although this may be the top of a much larger stone and further investigation is needed. It may be an ancient boundary stone or guide stone, like others found in the forest around Blidworth. However, the name suggests that it marks the centre of something. It is unlikely that it marks the centre of the estate as it does not appear to be in the correct position. It is more likely to have been the centre stone in a row or line of stones.

Although it does not appear in any history or on any map, the Centre Stone makes an appearance in local folklore. If local legend is to be believed, it played its part in the story of how Charles Beauclerk, the son of Charles II and Nell Gwynn, acquired the Bestwood Estate as the seat of the Dukes of St Albans. It is said to have been on the top of this stone that Nell dropped the last of a series of handkerchiefs on her perambulation of the boundaries of Bestwood Park. This legend suggests that the stone pre-dates the reign of Charles II (1630–1685). As there is no historical basis for Nell's exploits, could it be that the handkerchief-dropping story also pre-dates Charles's era and refers to an ancient boundary custom?

⚜ DIABOLICAL MISSILES: ⚜
'A BATTLE BETWEEN CHRISTIANITY AND PAGANISM'

The folklore of Britain is full of stories of the Devil, like some petulant child, throwing stones. His intended target is usually a Christian edifice. In most cases, these satanic missiles miss their target and land – with varying degrees of accuracy – harmlessly in the landscape. Here, they remain, proudly shown by generations of locals, as evidence of victory over the Devil.

Reasons for the Devil's attack vary, but most common are his indignation at the building of a new church or that he is offended by the sound of the church bells. One of the reasons why church bells are rung, other than to summon parishioners to service, is to ward off evil spirits

It is widely accepted by folklorists that such stories derive from the conflict between the early Christian Church and the native pagan religion it supplanted. Before the advent of the science of geology, these legends also served to explain the presence of such stones within the landscape.

The diabolic missiles generally fall into three categories: natural rock outcrops of local stone; 'glacial erratics', non-native stones deposited by retreating glaciers at the end of the last Ice Age 10,000 years ago; and 'worked stones' such as the remains of an ancient cross or a prehistoric monolith.

A number of counties have their examples of a diabolic missile, but Nottinghamshire is unique in possessing three. Chief of these is the Hemlock Stone at Bramcote which falls into the first category. The other examples, at Hickling and Kinoulton, are both glacial erratics.

⚜ The Hemlock Stone Legend ⚜

Our story starts not with the stone or its intended target, but with the Devil in Castleton, Derbyshire. Castleton takes its name from the Norman castle standing high on a hill above the town. At the foot of this hill is a natural limestone cave known as The Devil's Arse – because of the strange gurgling sounds that emanate from it after heavy rain. When this water flows from the cave, it is said to be the Devil urinating.

One fine summer's evening, before the castle existed, the Devil emerged from the underworld via the cave to take a stroll in the balmy evening air. He soon found himself at the top of the hill and here he lay down to enjoy the cooling breeze. Free from the cares of Hell, he drifted off into a deep sleep.

Thirty miles to the south, in Lenton Priory near Nottingham, a venerable old monk could not sleep. Sensing that the Devil was abroad, he paced his tiny cell wondering what he should do. Should he ring the chapel bell to alert his brother monks and the Father Abbott? Would they believe him?

With a heavy heart he sank to his knees in prayer, asking for God's guidance. Such was the piety of the monk that the power of his prayer ran through the ground like an electric current. It travelled in an instant to where the Devil lay and, like a bolt of lightning, entered his body through his cloven hooves.

The Devil awoke in a powerful rage and jumped to his feet. Seizing an enormous rock, he threw it with all his might in the direction from which the current had come. The stone whistled through the air and came to rest on a hillside at Bramcote to the west of the priory. The Devil had missed his target by over 4 miles.

It is said that from the moment the stone landed, the Devil has never slept and that the old monk fell into a deep sleep never to awake.

Putting an accurate date and origin on folk legends of this kind is usually difficult, if not impossible. However, the Hemlock Stone story may well be an exception. The authorship of the legend can be attributed to a monk of Lenton Priory and the date can therefore be no earlier than 1102–1108, the date of the founding of the priory.

The Hemlock Stone, a massive natural pillar of local sandstone, stood on the side of Stapleford Hill in Bramcote for tens of thousands of years before the priory. Over that time it had become the centre of pagan superstition and worship. The annual lighting of a bonfire on the top of the stone on May Day, the pagan Beltane, continued well into the seventeenth century.

The stone was on or close to regularly used routes between Lenton and two other monastic sites – Beauvale Priory and Dale (Abbey) Priory – and monks from all three establishments would have been familiar with the stone. We can imagine that monks would cross themselves or avert their eyes whenever they passed what to them was an obviouslu pagan and frightening object. As the biggest Christian influence in the area at this time, the authorities at Lenton would have needed to neutralise the pagan influences of the Hemlock Stone both on the monks and the local population. I believe that they achieved this in a tried and trusted way, by involving the stone in a story which demonstrated the power of the Christian Church over the old, the Devil.

The author of the tale displays a clear knowledge of all of the sites involved. The intended target of the Devil's missile, the old monk, has his dwelling at the priory and clearly stands for the power of the Church. Lenton Priory – for which there is evidence that it sits on a pre-Christian site – was founded by

Rudely awakened from his sleep, the Devil throws his missile. (Author's Illustration)

William Peverel. The site, from which the stone was thrown – the hill at Castleton in Derbyshire – appears not to have been chosen at random. Not only does it have a legend of an entrance to the underworld attached to it, but the castle on the hill was also founded by Peverel. Perhaps this is a subtle reference or acknowledgement to Peverel's lordship and his part in the defeat of Old Nick?

⚜ *The Hickling Legend* ⚜

Looking down from his lair on Hickling Standard, the Devil became increasingly angry as he watched the building of the church of St Luke in the village below. When at last the church was complete the priest began to ring the newly installed bell. To the Devil, this was the last straw.

A plan formed in the Devil's mind, and for weeks he avoided his lair on the hill. On the next night of a full moon, clutching a large boulder, he flew towards the church, intending to drop the stone on the church tower and destroy the offending bell.

St Peter, in Heaven, looked down on these events and decided that he must intervene. When the Devil was halfway between the church and Hickling Standard, he reached down and pulled the clouds over the face of the moon. Undeterred, the Devil flew on more determined than ever destroy the bell. St Peter waited until the Devil was close to his target and again reached down into the clouds. This time he pulled the clouds apart and the light of the moon shone straight into the Devil's eyes. With a scream that could be heard for miles, the Devil put his hands up to shield his eyes. In doing so he lost his grip on the stone and down it fell. Thwarted, he flew off into the night. Never again did he dare to return to Hickling Standard or to trouble the good Christians of the village.

The village of Hickling lies in the beautiful Vale of Belvoir, around 3 miles north-west of the A606 Melton Road. The road into the village – Bridgegate Lane – descends from the A606 past the hill known as Hickling Standard – a favourite haunt of the Devil. On the right-hand side of the crossroads between

The Devil on his bombing run. (Author's Illustration)

The Methodist chapel, Hickling, and the Hickling Stone. (Author's Photograph)

the Lane and Main Street is a curious boulder said to be evidence of the Devil's presence. This wedge-shaped stone – around 2ft tall, 3ft wide and 4ft long – is in fact a glacial erratic. In 1848, a Methodist chapel was built by the crossroads, but the stone was deliberately excluded from the churchyard. To this day it lies only inches from the enclosing wall.

⚛ *The Kinoulton Legend* ⚛

Perched on the hill where Lincoln Cathedral now stands, the Devil watched in alarm at the building of Kinoulton church. As day by day another course of stone was laid his anger grew. Finally, he could stand no more and he seized a large stone and with all his might threw it at the building. The stone missed its target by a matter of yards and landed on the north side – the Devil's quarter – of the churchyard. The failed sabotage did not deter the builders and the church was completed. The Devil never again tried to demolish it.

The parish church of St Wilfrid, Kinoulton, was built on a hill to the west, well outside the village. Churches built in such inconvenient places usually indicate that they were built on a pre-existing pagan site. The hill in question overlooks the village to the east and the Roman road, the Fosse Way, to the west. On the southern slope of the hill, close to the modern road, maps indicate the presence of a spa or healing spring. On the north side of the churchyard was a large stone, probably a glacial erratic. Given all of these factors it is reasonable to suspect that the site of the church was a pagan shrine or sanctuary, possibly the stone itself.

St Wilfred's church was considered to be too remote from the village and by the late 1700s it had fallen into ruin. The roof was removed and it was finally demolished in 1792, shortly after the new red-brick church was built in the village. The Devil's missile was broken up and used for road mending.

DOWNE (ROBIN): A LIFE AND DEATH ON THE MANSFIELD ROAD

Almost opposite Mansfield's Municipal Cemetery, Sanderson's 1835 Map marks a small eminence as 'Robin Downs Hill' – now Berry Hill and Robin Down Lane. The name is not an ancient one and dates to an incident in 1767 involving the unfortunate young man Robin Downe. Robin would have been a familiar sight around Mansfield. He was a young man with learning   difficulties, who travelled around playing the flute and begging.

Georgian England was full of unfortunates like Robin. Without a proper welfare system the old and disabled who had no family support were forced to wander from parish to parish begging. However, those in genuine need were hindered by the great number of what might be termed professional beggars. Some years earlier, in 1725, the author of *A New Canting Dictionary* states that 'no country in the world abounds so much with vagrants and beggars'.

Most people treated Robin kindly and considered him a harmless fool; however, he could lose his temper when provoked. One fine summer morning Robin was wondering along the road towards Mansfield, playing his flute as usual. He was not alone on the road however. A group of younger boys were following along behind Robin, teasing him and calling him names.

One of the boys, a deaf mute by the name of Thomas Greenwood, egged on by the others, was being particularly annoying. A scuffle ensued and a knife was pulled from Robin's pocket. The result was that Greenwood was stabbed to death.

(Author's Collection)

Robin was arrested and taken for trial in Nottingham. The jury wanted to acquit Robin on the grounds of what we would now call 'diminished responsibility'. However, the judge decided to put Robin to the test by offering him two coins, a large silver crown and a much smaller gold sovereign. He reasoned that if Robin was indeed a halfwit, he would take the larger coin, believing it to be of greater value. However, after some slight hesitation, Robin chose the gold coin. The judge decided that this was an indication that he knew the value of money and was therefore no idiot. He informed the jury of his decision and instructed them to find him guilty of a capital offence.

Robin was sentenced to death and duly executed on the gallows on 10 August 1767. It is probable that given the date, the place of execution was Gallows Hill on the Mansfield Road just outside Nottingham, around where Rock Cemetery gates now stand. At this time Gallows Hill was the city's main site for executions which were performed in public. Robin's body was cut down and ordered to be hung in chains by the side of the road at the Gravel Pits, Lichfield Road, near Mansfield. The spot became known as Robin Down(s) Hill.

$\mathcal{E}$

❧ EGYPTIAN NIGHTJAR (THE): ❧
THE GAMEKEEPER AND THE GENTLEMAN

Around 10 miles north of Nottingham's city centre, along the west side of Mansfield Road (A60) is Thieves Wood. Once a part of Sherwood Forest, the name denotes the time when it was once the notorious haunt of robbers who frequented the area. Within the wood – now a public space – is perhaps one of the county's strangest monuments, the Bird Stone. The stone commemorates an event in 1883 which history might otherwise have overlooked, if it had not been for the timely intervention of Joseph Whitaker.

Joseph Whitaker was a gentleman of independent means and one of Victorian Nottinghamshire's eccentric characters. He lived for most of his life at Rainworth Lodge, a house around one mile east of Thieves Wood and the stone. As well as a comfortable living, Joseph had inherited from his father a love of the outdoors and natural history. A keen botanist and fisherman, the inside of Rainworth Lodge resembled a museum, containing cases of stuffed birds and other natural history exhibits. He also had his own deer park and collection of deer antlers. Joseph also had a passion for sports and was one of the sponsors of the Nottingham prize fighter Bendigo. He also indulged himself in writing and publishing rather bad poetry and it is perhaps fortunate that he is not remembered for his verse. However, in 1927 he went on to publish a book on Nottinghamshire's medieval dovecotes. Although regarded as partially inaccurate – a number of his examples are outside the county – this work inspired a more modern survey by the Nottinghamshire Building Preservation Trust.

Gamekeeper Albert Spinks lived in a small cottage in Harlow Wood, just south of Thieves Wood, opposite the Bessie Sheppherd Stone. To say that Spinks and Whitaker were friends is perhaps an over-statement, but given Spinks's job and Whitaker's interest, it is certain that they were acquaintances.

On the morning of 23 June 1883, Spinks was out shooting rabbits. He fired and missed his target, but the sound of the shot put to flight a medium-sized brown bird. With the second barrel of his shotgun, Spinks instinctively fired again, hitting the bird. On recovering the animal, he found it to be a species he did not recognise. By one of those strange, chance coincidences, before he had disposed of the body,

Spinks met Whitaker and mentioned the incident. Fortunately, Joseph was able to identify the bird as an Egyptian Nightjar.

Whitaker went on to have the body of the unfortunate bird stuffed and mounted. It can now be seen as a part of the Whitaker Collection of exhibits at the Mansfield Museum and Art Gallery and can be viewed by appointment. On the spot where Spinks had shot the bird, Whitaker placed a memorial stone with an inscription recording Spinks's unusual sighting. However, this fails to note the fact that Spinks had shot the bird. The stone was badly damaged by vandals in the 1980s. It was replaced by a more enigmatic memorial, a stone plinth with an engraved stylised bird and simply the date, 1883.

An Egyptian Nightjar, *caprimulgus aegyptius*. Joseph Whitaker's original specimen. (Author's Collection)

As the name implies, the Egyptian Nightjar is a desert-dwelling species from Egypt and parts of North Africa. How it came to be in a Nottinghamshire wood is a mystery. The bird is so rare to Europe that Spinks's sighting is one of only two in Britain. The second sighting was just over a hundred years later in Dorset on 10 June 1984. Fortunately, this time it was by a bird spotter with a camera and not a gamekeeper with a gun and the bird survived the encounter.

⁑ FAITH HEALING: ⁑
THE STROKING BOY OR WISE CHILD OF WYSALL

In 1623, ecclesiastical records indicate that something strange was occurring in the Nottinghamshire village of Wysall. Around Michaelmas – 29 September, one of the cross-quarter days – there appears the first reference to the fact that Wysall had become a place of pilgrimage for those wishing to see the wise boy, also known as the 'stroking boy'. Given the title, it is reasonable to surmise that here was a young man who claimed healing powers and perhaps rendered his cures by stroking the patient. Those making the pilgrimage were therefore desperate people seeking a cure for themselves or a loved one.

A Presentation Bill (an indictment) put before court at West Bridgford is headed: 'West Bridgford of Richard Garton, husbandman, for carrying his child to Wysall to be cured by the "stroking boy".'

The Church authorities were so concerned by the activities of the stroking boy that they issued an order to a number of parishes to submit the names of those who had visited the child: 'The names of those that by report and fame went to the child at Wisall' [Wysall]…but of our own knowledge we cannot say.' The records include seven parishes: 'Broughton Sulney an Ane' (Broughton Solney), West Bridgford, Wollaton, Trowell, Costock, Lenton and East Leake. Also included is the hamlet of Bassingfield. It is not clear if this list is comprehensive or whether these are the only references to survive. It may be that only these parishes were questioned because the authorities already had their suspicions. It may be noted that the question asks for the names of those visiting the stroking boy of which the authority has no knowledge, implying that it already had knowledge of others. Of the parishes questioned, the returns were as follows:

Broughton Sulney an Ane: Brett, Edward Weston and his wife; Thomas Lister with his son and Margerie Frances, and William Hemsley; 'for going to the boy at Wysall'.

West Bridgford: Elizabeth Harding, wife of Walter Harding of Bridgford; Jone Seemons, wife of Michaell Seemons of Bassingfeild; Katherine Whitworth, wife of Reginald Whitworth of Bridgford; Anne Wright, Marie Dauson, Elizabeth Coopers and Isabell Hilton of Bridgford; '… going to and seeking unlawful means of help from the stroking boy who was at Wisall [sic].'

Seeking the stroking boy. (Author's Illustration)

Without doubt the powers of the stroking boy must have been considered remarkable and amongst the submissions we find reports from the parishes of Wollaton and Trowel, both a considerable walking distance from Wysall.

From Wollaton: Elline Bruchouse, Ellizabeth Simmones, Elline Browne, and Alles Skeletonm 'for going to the wise boy'.

From Trowell: Gabriel Eaton and Nicholas Lansdale, 'for resorting to the boy at Wysall, commonly called the wise child and for being touched of the said child in hope of some miraculous healing, contrary, as they are persuaded, to God's word and the ecclesiastical laws.'

This last entry gives a clear picture of the whole story of the stroking boy. First it gives an alternative name by which he was known – 'commonly called the wise child'. Secondly, it tells us why people travelled miles to consult with him: 'in hope of some miraculous healing'. Thirdly, it tells how he might have effected a cure 'for being touched of the said child'. Finally, it tells us the attitude of the Church, 'contrary, as they are persuaded, to God's word and the ecclesiastical laws.'

From Costock: 'concerning any that were supposed to go to the child at Wysall for any manner of cure, they cannot find any.'

Lenton and East Leake do not appear to have submitted a return. However, this does not mean that no one from these parishes visited the stroking boy, only that there were no names to be submitted. Perhaps the records have been lost, or could it be that those who had visited Wysall from these parishes were already known to the authorities?

A total of twenty-three people from four parishes are recorded as visiting the stroking boy. Of these more than half (thirteen) were women. All of these individuals pleaded guilty to breaking Church law, however none were ever formally charged and all were subsequently dismissed. There is no evidence that the stroking boy was ever charged with any offence and no mention of him in the records of 1624 and thereafter. Did he escape detection, or was the Church satisfied that he was of no threat to their authority?

❧ FLYING CARS AND FLYING BEDSTEADS ❧

This is my chance to put together a story my father once told me when I was a child. I have no way of independently verifying it, but as facts and circumstance seem to fit, in all likelihood it is true.

For reasons which will become apparent, the incident must have occurred sometime between 3 August and 15 December 1954. One morning, sometime between the mid and later part of this period, my father was working in the garden of my grandfather's farm at Halfway House, Wollaton. It was a still morning when the sound carried from some distance away, of a distant roar of a jet engine, drew his attention skyward. Looking to the north he saw a strange object hovering at treetop height in the sky above Hucknall a little under 4 miles away. He had never before seen such an object and immediately rushed into the house to inform the rest of the family. As soon as he entered the old farmhouse kitchen, he declared that he had seen a 'flying car' and called upon all those present to come outside to see for themselves. By the time everyone was out in the garden, the UFO had disappeared.

My father's strange sighting of a flying car was greeted by the family with incredulity and some good humour. But the disbelief was soon dropped and the mystery solved when the newspapers announced that there had been testing of a new aircraft at the Rolls-Royce test centre at Hucknall Aerodrome. Accompanying pictures showed this to be my father's UFO, his flying car.

The Rolls-Royce Thrust Measuring Rig (TMR), or as it was more familiarly known the Flying Bedstead, was in fact like no other conventional aircraft ever trialled. It consisted of two Rolls-Royce Nene turbojet engines, mounted back to back horizontally and set within a steel frame (the rig), which in turn was mounted on four legs with castors for wheels. The pilot sat in an open cockpit, set directly over the engines, at about mid-point along the rig. The basic oblong shape, four legs and the fact that it was totally without wings or rotors as lifting surfaces, meant that it quickly gained the nickname of the Flying Bedstead. Personally, I think that in some photos and illustrations, the TMR resembles an old-fashioned open-topped sports car and my father's flying car analogy is a good one.

The TMR, largely the work of Dr Alan Griffith, was a pioneering rig to test the potential of vertical take-off technology. The first test flight was carried out at Hucknall on 19 July 1954, with the machine tethered to a gantry. Over the following month, several more successful tethered test flights were made. Piloted by Captain Ron Shepherd, the TMR made its first free flight on 3 August 1953, in the presence of a distinguished audience. The rig rose slowly into the air to the height of around 12ft to 15ft where it hovered for a while before making a circuit of the test area. After demonstrating sideways and backwards movement, it returned to earth, making a successful landing. During the next four months a number of further free flights were made all to the same height. However, one flight – likely to be the one my father witnessed – was made to the height of 50ft. The final flight was made on 15 December 1954, before the rig was taken to Farnborough for further work. A second test rig was built and tethered flights – beginning on 17 October 1955 – continued successfully for a year. This rig made its first free flight on 12 November 1956, but it crashed a year later on 28 November 1957, killing the test pilot. Further testing of the TMR ceased at the Rolls-Royce test centre at Hucknall. The success of the test flights of the TMR led to the development of the Rolls-Royce RB 108 direct-lift turbojet, five of which were used to power the first true British VTOL aircraft, the Short, which first took to the air in the late 1950s.

G

❧ GHOSTS ❧

Charlie, the Halfway House Ghost

I was born in the haunted bedroom of a haunted house called Halfway House. Not that I ever experienced anything of the phenomenon. I have many happy childhood memories there. The only 'spooky' thing was the occasions when one of my two older cousins tried to frighten me by playing – badly – on the organ in the front room; a place strictly out of bounds for younger members of the family, with all the best furniture and two giant glass showcases full of stuffed birds, acquired somehow from Wollaton Hall – it was my grandmother's pride and joy.

Halfway House was a large rambling building close to the canal on Woodyard Lane, Wollaton. It had once been a part of the Middleton Estate. My research shows that its name was derived from the fact that it was halfway between Wollaton Hall and Aspley Hall.

A 1950s photograph of Halfway House. (Author's Photograph)

The house was semi-detached and over the years I have often wondered if the neighbours ever experienced any of the supernatural activity. My chance to find out came recently when I was contacted by members of the neighbouring family after I had published an article on the ghost. Apparently, that side of the house was free from any form of haunting.

There was no gas or electricity and only a single cold water tap in the small scullery. The toilet, next to the pigsty 100 yards from the house, was a seat over a large tub which was emptied weekly by the night soil men.

My grandparents and their young family had moved into the house in the 1930s. My father's bedroom – the one in which I was born – was at the front of the house, with a view towards the canal. He was one of the first to experience something of the activity, waking on occasions to find his large iron bed had moved over 3ft from the wall.

By the time I came on the scene, the ghost, who the family nicknamed 'Charlie', was an established part of the family. My grandfather seemed to know when things would happen. 'Go to sleep early tonight,' he would say, 'Charlie is walking.' These nocturnal ramblings seem to have been limited to three to four occasions a year, one of which was around three nights before Christmas.

The focus of the activity seemed to be the hall and stairs and the front bedroom. Things began with the sound of slow footsteps on the stairs – 'like someone in carpet-slippers' witnesses would say – and the sound of a hand rubbing against the wall.

The noise would reach the top of the stairs, there was a pause, and then, from the door an intense black, formless shadow would enter the room. Slowly, this would spread and the air become oppressive. As it reached the bed witnesses said that you could not avert your eyes and it felt as if a great weight was pushing down upon your body, making it impossible to move. If the candle was lit on the bedside table, as the darkness passed over, it would splutter and the flame would burn low.

Slowly, as the darkness passed through the room, the original light intensity would return. Witnesses would be released from its spell and the candle would flare back to its former brightness. The darkness left the room through the 'partition wall' by the window. I was later to discover that on the other side of this wall was a small room – my father described it as an apple store – which once connected both sides of the house. As the last trace exited, the whole room returned to normal. It was all over until the next time Charlie walked.

For a time, my aunt and uncle – my mother's sister – occupied the downstairs front room as a sort of bedsit. As far as I am aware this was the first time the room had been used as a bedroom. As a teenager, I overheard my father and uncle discussing Charlie's Christmas visit. My uncle was earnestly describing how events that we originally believed began with footsteps on the stairs, actually started in their room.

My aunt and uncle were sitting talking by the light of a storm lamp – fortunately, my cousins were asleep. Without warning, silently a black mass began to rise from the floor at the centre of the room. It had the same effect on them as those who had witnessed the events in the bedroom. The darkness began to fill the room – almost as a column. Although the flame was covered by glass, the light of the lamp was almost extinguished as the darkness engulfed it. Slowly, the mass moved towards the door to the hall and stairs. As it passed through the door, the light of the lamp flooded back. For a few seconds, there was silence, and then the sound of footsteps and a hand on the wall as Charlie ascended the stairs.

The Railway Ghost

As well as working on the farm with my grandfather, my father had various other jobs. For a time he worked for British Rail as part of a 'maintenance gang'. One cold and frosty morning he found himself in the old 'lines man's hut' on the stretch of line a field away from Halfway House. Sitting with a colleague enjoying a freshly brewed cup of tea, my father distinctly heard the sound of heavy footsteps approaching the hut. Thinking it was a fellow worker coming to join them, my father – who was nearest the door – got up and opened it. Peering out in both directions he could see no one. The instant he closed the door – before he could return to his seat – the sound began again. Thinking that this was some practical joke, my father instantly opened the door and rushed out onto the track. The morning air was silent except for bird song and there was no one to be seen. The process continued for several minutes with my father opening and closing the door – door closed footsteps, door open no footsteps. Finally, the door was closed and my father sat down and the sound stopped. His colleague, an old hand – then explained that this was a regular occurrence on such a morning. If ignored, the footsteps continued for a few minutes and then stopped, but never seemed to get any closer to the hut.

The Wollaton Colliery Ghost

By the time I was born, my father was working as a 'faceworker' at the nearby Wollaton Colliery. The pit had been in operation from the 1800s and there were a number of abandoned and disused workings. One of these, a flooded 'road', was supposedly haunted. This took the form of the sight of a miner's helmet lamp approaching the witness, accompanied by the sound of splashing footsteps through the water. Like the railway hut ghost, the sound and sight never seemed to get any closer. Miners are stoic fellows and are not easily frightened, however my father witnessed one poor chap almost scared out of his wits. Returning to the surface after a shift, my father was with a group which included a miner who had transferred from another pit. Passing the old workings, like naughty schoolboys they dared the new man to go along the tunnel. Leaving the well-lit road, without hesitation, the man boldly disappeared along the tunnel into the darkness. He returned over 5 minutes later looking shaken and frightened. He refused to say what he had seen and vowed never to enter the abandoned section again, even if ordered to do so by management.

The Bramcote Ghost

All that remains of the medieval church of St Michael in Bramcote is the square tower. Popularly known as the Sunken Church, the tower within the remains of the churchyard stands high above Town Street, almost opposite its junction with Cow Lane. In 1978, a motorist driving by the church reported seeing a black hooded figure, which he described as 'monk like', in the churchyard. Later the same year, a police officer driving the same route reported seeing a similar figure. Though no further reports of sightings of the ghost have been mentioned, driving past the site and the old church can be an eerie experience, especially on a moonlit night.

A phantom monk or guardian spirit? (Author's Illustration)

The Calverton Ghost

From Nottingham, the ancient road into the village of Calverton begins in Arnold as Calverton Road. It passes north over the hill known as Dorket Head and crosses the B684 – Lime Lane, Woodborough Road. From this junction, it takes the name Georges Lane. For just over one mile, Georges Lane snakes its way over the wooded Georges Hill and descends into the village where it terminates at Main Street. Georges Lane has become infamous for its hauntings. It is said that taxi drivers will avoid using this route into the village. On a dark winter's night, the lane, particularly in the wooded section, seems to generate an air of terror. On a number of occasions this has been manifested by an actual presence. Several motorists have reported seeing in their rearview mirror an elderly lady sitting in the back of their vehicle and at least one reported seeing a hooded figure. These phantoms usually disappear when the driver attempts to investigate their presence further. A young student returning home one evening was shaken when her car struck a dark figure that ran out in front of the vehicle. Stopping the car, she got out, expecting to find an injured pedestrian lying in the road. However, she could see no one and so she ran home to get help. Although she returned with her father and searched the area by torchlight, no trace of an accident was found.

The earliest recorded report of the strange haunting on Georges Lane comes from the 1930s. At around midnight, a young man by the name of Bardhill encountered a strange and frightening entity whilst walking home from the Goose Fair. He had reached the point where Georges Lane begins at Dorket Head, when he saw a dark mass emerge from the hedge bottom on the left-hand side of the road. Mr Bardhill, keeping an eye on the 'things', continued walking. He quickly realised that it was keeping pace with him and as it did so changed into the form of a tall man wearing what seemed to be a cloak and a broad-brimmed hat. Around the figure's shoulders he could clearly see a large silver chain. Although Mr Bardhill could not make out his companion's features, he could discern a large hooked nose. The figure appeared to glide rather than walk and effortlessly paralleled Mr Bardhill's course, even when he had quickened his pace and crossed to the other side of the road. Understandably, Mr Bardhill became very alarmed and began to run, pursued at a short distance by the sinister figure. It was not until he neared the village and home that the phantom disappeared back into the hedge. Mr Bardhill eventually arrived home in a very distressed state and reported feeling unwell for a number of days after the event. A number of years later, the wife of a local farmer was driving along Georges Lane at around dusk. In the rearview mirror she could clearly see a figure – which matched the one described by Mr Bardhill – sitting in the back of her car. The unwanted passenger stayed with the unfortunate lady all the way to the village where it disappeared as she turned into her drive.

The Georges Hill ghost. Reminiscent of the Norse god Odin or Saxon Woden, is this apparition the first appearance of 'Hat Man'? (Author's Illustration)

Footnote:

Since the 1930s, sighting of the strange figure in the broad-brimmed hat, a similar apparition has made an appearance all over the world. So common are the reported sightings that the ghost has been given the name 'Hat Man'. It may be that Hat Man is an imprint on the popular mind of the 'Freddy Krueger' character from the 1980s film franchise, *A Nightmare on Elm Street*. However, at Calverton he is something far older. The description of the Calverton ghost is almost identical to the Norse god Odin, aka Grimmer. His appearance at Calverton is on a site close to Grim's Moor, which is believed to take its name from Woden.

Gotham's Naked Man

December 1976 saw the village of Gotham covered with a light blanket of snow. On a cold and frosty night, just before Christmas, Fred Talbot – a respected member of the community, whose family had lived in the village for generations – set out to meet his friends for his weekly game of whist. Fred took his usual shortcut through the churchyard. Here, he was to encounter a frightening apparition. Gliding between the tombstones and keeping a parallel course to his, he saw what he later described as a spectral figure of a wild-looking man. However, this wasn't the usual hooded phantom. The man was naked and Fred was later to state that his manhood was decidedly prominent. Keeping the figure in sight, Fred retreated from the churchyard as quickly as possible and arrived at his destination visibly shaken.

Rufford's Terrifying Monk and Spectral Hound

Rufford Abbey is said to be one of the most haunted sites in Nottinghamshire. Founded in the twelfth century as a Cistercian priory, during the Dissolution it became a country house. At one time it was the estate of the Byron family who added their own mystery and romance to the place. It finally passed to the Savile family in whose hands it remained until 1938. It is now a country park with the remains of the priory and the house managed by English Heritage.

The house is most famously haunted by a ghost known as the 'White Lady', a spectre encountered by Lord Byron (the poet) himself. Within the grounds, allegedly on the site of the high altar of the priory church, is the grave of Byron's faithful hound, Boatswain. The monument is inscribed with a touching verse by Byron. The spot is said to be the haunt of a spectral black dog with shining red eyes. Is this the ghost of Boatswain, or something much older?

British folklore records a number of cases of spectral black dogs with shining red eyes. They are usually associated with lonely crossroads or stretches of isolated roads and sometimes ancient prehistoric sites. Folklorists attribute such animals as being the guardian spirit of the place. In rare examples, the black dog is encountered in the presence of its master. Could this be the case in our next Newstead ghost, the Black Friar?

A number of people have encountered the Black Friar whilst walking in the grounds. He appears as a tall, hooded figure with a skeletal face. He is said to come upon people from behind and tap them on the shoulder'. In the early 1900s, the Friar's actions are believed to have literally frightened a man to death. There are a number such phantom monks in the county but Rufford is perhaps the best known and most frightening.

Newstead has many more examples of ghostly happenings that remain largely unknown to the public. Examples include a phantom car that never reaches its destination, a herd of deer seen by the lake, and, on one sunny morning, a monk in a brown habit seen digging with a spade in a hedgerow.

⁂ GOOSE FAIR ⁂

'He that eats goose on Michaelmas Day,
shan't money lack or debts to pay.'

Anon.

There are two birds which feature large in the folklore of Nottinghamshire, the cuckoo and the goose. Of the two, it is perhaps the goose which is dearest to the hearts of the good folk of Nottingham, young and old. The goose is the symbol of the much celebrated and world-famous Goose Fair. In the week before the arrival of the fair, the erection of a large fibreglass figure of the bird, on the traffic island at the junction of Gregory Boulevard and Mansfield Road, always creates great excitement in the city. The Goose Fair – at least in name – has been held almost continuously for over 400 years, but its origins are believed to be much older and there has been a fair held around the same date since Saxon times.

Traditional origin: local legend tells how there was once a fisherman on the iver Trent. After fishing for a while and catching a few carp and other fish, his bait was taken by a monster pike. For some time, man and fish struggled in that conflict enjoyed by anglers. Eventually, the great fish tired and the man began to reel it towards the shore. At that moment – as the fish began to emerge from the water – a wild goose flying overhead swooped down and seized the fish in its beak. The goose flew high into the air with its prize, but the pike still had the baited hook in its mouth and the man still held tight to his rod. Imagine the scene when the goose flew over Nottingham's market square with pike, rod and man dangling from its beak! The burden was too much for the bird and it released its grip. Down tumbled the angler, rod and fish. The astonished crowd rushed to the man's aid, only to find him standing unhurt in the middle of the square – he had landed safely on his feet. In celebration of this wonderful event it was decided to hold a fair on the very spot where the man had landed and it was to be known as the Goose Fair.

This tale purports to be the origin of the Goose Fair, but is, of course, just a charming folk tale. So, what is the true origin of the fair? The clue is in its name and the time of year at which it is held – a Michaelmas Fair.

Michaelmas, or more correctly the Feast of St Michael and All Angels, is celebrated on 29 September (in Suffolk it is marked on 4 October and in Norfolk 11 October). It marks the first day of the new farming year and is one of the four 'quarter days' – 25 March, Lady Day, 24 June, Midsummer's Day, 29 September, Michaelmas, and 25 December, Christmas. These dates are close to an equinox or solstice in the solar calendar and make up the divisions of the agricultural year.

Michaelmas also marks the end of the harvest season and many of the fairs held at this time were Hiring Fairs where labourers finished with the harvest would seek employment for the winter.

Often, folklore stories have embedded in them a sort of coded message or truth. I have puzzled over the story of the fisherman, the pike and the goose, in order to understand what it might mean. The 29 September also marks the end of the fishing season and the start of the hunting season. Is the story a salutary warning not to fish beyond this date? The wild goose might indicate that the man should turn his attention to the hunt. Again, in ancient tradition and folklore the wild goose in flight has strong associations with hunting dogs, particularly those of the Wild Hunt.

A version of the Wild Hunt occurs in many cultures but the features of the story are always the same; a hero or god-like figure – a psychopomp, the conductor of the dead to the 'Other World' – leads a pack of spectral hounds across the sky. Their quarry is the souls of those about to die. In Christianity, St Michael is recognised as a psychopomp and has connections to the wild goose.

The word fair comes from the Latin *feria*, meaning a holy day, defined as a time when a large number of people would assemble for worship. Fairs were held annually on the Feast Day of a saint, which in turn often marked a special time of year within the calendar.

Very quickly the Church realised that fairs were a great opportunity to make money through commerce and trade, and fairs quickly developed into markets, often lasting for several days. So lucrative to their sponsors were these markets, they could only be held under a grant of a Royal Charter.

In medieval Europe, fairs were held in the precincts of the great monastic houses and individual churchyards. However, in England the venue was left to the discretion of the authorities and fairs were often held on village greens and other open spaces.

The earliest reference to a fair in Nottingham – St Mathew's Fair, 21 September – comes from Saxon times. A charter to hold a Martinmas Fair on 11 November was granted by Henry II, to the Priory of Lenton in 1164. This ran for eight days and was extended to twelve days sometime in the thirteenth century. The charter forbade the holding of any other fair or market in the district during this time and so eclipsed all other fairs in Nottingham. Lenton Fair continued up until the Dissolution in 1536 but is still mentioned in Harrisons Calendar of Fairs in 1587.

Charters were not exclusive to the Church and individual towns were granted the privilege to hold a fair. In 1284 the burgesses of Nottingham were granted a charter by Edward I, to hold a fair on the eve of the Feast of St Edmund – 20 November – and for twelve days following. We can see how, when Lenton Fair was extended, these fairs might have clashed.

Nottingham's Goose Fair is first recorded by name in the borough records of 1541. Removed from the restrictions and competition of Lenton Fair, the Goose Fair flourished in Tudor times. Although the date for the fair was set at 21 September – and for eight days following, reduced to three in 1800 – an eleven-day change to the calendar in 1751 meant that it is now held on the first week in October.

Goose Fair became famous as a cheese fair but it is the Michaelmas Goose which is remembered and marked in its name. Geese hatched in the spring were ready for the table by Michaelmas and it became customary, for those able to afford it, to celebrate with a meal of a well-fattened goose. It was also customary for tenants to present their landlords, in part payment of rent, with a fine brace of geese.

The twenty-first century Goose Fair. (Courtesy of Joe Earp)

Geese for the Michaelmas market were driven into Nottingham from Lincolnshire. Preparations for the long walk started with tar being applied to the birds' feet. It is recorded that anything up to 20,000 geese were driven up through Hockley and along Goose Gate into the market square.

By the early nineteenth century, Goose Fair had largely developed from a trade fair (market) into a fun fair. By 1927 the fair had outgrown the confines of the square. The following year it was moved to its current home, the Forest Recreation Ground. Showmen from all over the country have annually brought their entertainments to Nottingham and the fair has become the largest travelling fair (non-permanent) in Europe.

Although it is always stated that the fair has been continuously held throughout its history, there have been at least three events which caused its cancellation. In 1646, the fair was cancelled due to outbreaks of bubonic plague. In the twentieth century the fair was not held during the years of the two world wars (1914–18 and 1939–45).

When next you visit Nottingham's Goose Fair, remember its long history and if you want to have money in your pocket to spend whilst you are there, remember the old adage and eat your goose on Michaelmas Day!

⚜ GROVES ⚜

Clifton Grove

> 'Dear native grove, where'er my devious track
> To thee will memory lead the wanderer back.
> Still, still to thee where'er my footsteps roam,
> My heart shall point, and lead the wanderer home.'

Henry Kirk White

Many Nottingham people have fond memories of Clifton Grove. Perhaps as children they played in the woods or on the grass of the long straight drive. Building dens among the trees, or swinging out dangerously on ropes tied to a branch. Or when they were older, memories of picnicking on a summer's afternoon, or simply taking a leisurely walk, hand in hand with the one they love. Those with such memories are in good company. The Grove has been a popular attraction for the people of Nottingham for well over 200 years and remains so. 'Down the Grove and Witches Steps!' is still a popular saying among Clifton folk. It seems that you can't help waxing lyrical when dealing with Clifton's famous Grove.

So what is The Grove and why has it attracted so much attention? It is in fact not a grove in the strictest sense of the word, but a wide grass track or lane, lined on both sides with trees and shrubs. The track begins on the south bank of the River Trent close to Clifton Bridge. Travelling west, it crosses the Fairham Brooke, where once was an ancient bridge. It then climbs to the top of the sandstone cliffs that form the south bank of the river and follows their line to the gates of Clifton Hall.

In 1677, Sir William Clifton planted the famous avenue of elm trees on either side of the track, to make it more suitable as an approach or drive to the hall. More trees were added in the 1740s. Sadly, many of the stately trees were lost in the 1970s during an outbreak of Dutch elm disease.

It is clear that the track was not originally created by the Clifton family as the drive to the hall as some writers suggest, but was merely adopted as such. There is strong evidence that it was part of a prehistoric trackway and a long established public right of way.

Where it begins to climb to the cliff top, aerial photos of the large field between the track and the river show the paleo-channel of the Trent. Alongside this, on the old south bank (Clifton side) are the shadowy outlines of several Bronze Age ring ditches and what appears to be the earlier course of the track.

The highest point along the cliff line – once marked by a large conglomerate boulder – is known as Lovers Leap. It is said to be the spot where Margaret, the tragic Fair Maid of Clifton, threw herself into the foaming waters of the Trent.

The track terminates in a large area of planted woodland on the eastern side of the hall. Although this wood is relatively modern, it is reputed to be the site of an ancient oak grove, long associated with the Druids. This is clearly the origin of the name Grove.

In the seventeenth and eighteenth centuries this wood became the back garden or pleasure ground to the hall. Careful exploration of the woods will reveal the remains of formal planting, a fountain, shooting lodge and, close by the river, a pump house.

Also within the wood are the Witches Steps, a short flight of stairs descending the steepest part of the slope towards the river. There appears to be no ancient tradition as to how the steps got their name. An oral tradition has it that generations of local children have heard the sound of mocking, cackling laughter coming from behind them whilst descending the steps. In reality, the Witches Steps appear to be the access to part of the Trent known as Colonel Clifton's Pool.

The whole course of the track which constitutes the Grove is around two miles long. However, a series of footpaths continue to follow the high ground above the river for around four miles to the confluence of the River Soar at Red Hill (close by Ratcliff on Soar Power Station). On the crown of the hill 2,000 years ago was a Roman temple dedicated to the goddess Minerva, now believed to have been surrounded by a temple complex and small town.

If we look more carefully at this possible Roman connection, a more positive pattern begins to emerge. The ancient ford which gives the village of Wilford its name has been identified as being in use in Roman times (although it may have had an earlier origin). On the Nottingham side of the ford a track can be traced leading down to the river. Where this track meets the sandstone ridge upon which the city stands joins two of Nottingham's most ancient roads, Hollow Stone and Stony Street (the latter identified by its name as a possible Roman Road).

By the time the Clifton family began to develop their garden wood, the Grove was already a popular public walk for the folk of Nottingham. Whenever the weather permitted, hundreds of people would cross the river via the Wilford ferry and walk the length of the Grove to Clifton village. Clifton had a Maypole, a possible turf maze, tea shops catering for the visitors and the newly developed woodland at the hall end of the Grove. There were also games and sports on the village green.

Clifton and its Grove did not just appeal to the older generation of Nottingham. Teenagers and young people flocked to this side of the Trent to, as one writer at the time put it, 'spend the day in merry pastimes on the village green and walking the length of Clifton Grove'. Not everyone in Clifton approved of these activities. Complaints were made by some of the villagers to local government about the 'noise, nuisance and lateness of those returning home in the evening'. At this time, the Clifton family tried, unsuccessfully, to prevent public access to the Grove. It is at this point that we have proof that the Grove was an ancient public trackway with established right of access

Old postcard showing the nineteenth-century popularity of Clifton Grove. (Courtesy of the Paul Nix Collection)

(and perhaps the wood too). Had it not been so, then isn't it likely that the family would have simply gated-off their drive?

By the nineteenth century the Grove had become the most popular retreat from the rigours of Nottingham. Shaw's *Guide to Nottingham* from 1874 states: 'At Easter and Whitsuntide if the weather at all permits, thousands of Nottingham artizans with their wives and families, and young men and maidens, either with sweethearts or to gain sweethearts, flock to the Grove.'

Whatever the attractions, the Grove has always been a romantic spot and place for lovers, as attested to by the Nottinghamshire poet Henry Kirk White (1783–1806). Henry suffered from tuberculosis, a condition from which he died at an early age. At the age of 17 he spent a month convalescing from his illness. Henry chose to live in the village of Wilford and spent time penning some of his greatest lines in a little gazebo which stood in the churchyard. As part of his recuperation he would have spent time walking the Grove to Clifton. Taking in fresh air was once considered a cure for tuberculosis. Here he would have heard the ancient legend of The Fair Maid, and been inspired to publish his first volume of poems, which includes 'The Fair Maid of Clifton and Clifton Grove'.

Radford Grove

> 'There is a spot of earth supremely blest.
> A dear and sweater spot than all the rest.'
>
> *Henry Sutton*

It is hard to imagine Radford as anything other than what it is today – a large suburb of Nottingham with all the associated attributes of such an area. Within my lifetime, Radford was a place thriving with industry – including some of Nottingham's well-known names – Players and Raleigh. Along with these sites – rows of terrace houses, pubs, shops, a railway station, colliery, cinema, and several textile factories. This was the world of author Alan Sillitoe. With time and 'progress' much of this has now disappeared.

Strictly speaking, however, most of this area was counted as New Radford and Radford Woodhouse, which only came into being in 1850. The earliest reference to the village of Radford comes from the Domesday Book of 1086, where it appears as the Anglo-Saxon village of Redeford – literally 'the red ford'. The name is derived from the place where the road on the north side of the village – now Alfreton Road – crossed the River Leen. This ford was flanked on one side by a high 'red' sandstone cliff. A second ford existed on the south side at the bottom end of St Peters Street, where Ilkeston Road crosses the river. The medieval village developed as a cluster of houses around the ford and the church of St Peter.

The earliest medieval reference to Radford – 'the Outgoings of Radford' – comes from 1488. Over the centuries, the earlier buildings were replaced with more substantial dwellings and by 1914 the oldest building, with the exception of the church, was the White Horse public house which had a date of 1661.

By 1790 the village appears to be in a state of some decline. St Peter's church is described as being in a 'ruinous state'. The church continued in this way for a further twenty years until 1810 to 1812 when it was largely rebuilt at the cost of £2,000. A new chancel was added much later in 1877.

In St Peter's churchyard is the grave of William Elliot, who died in 1792. He was the man who bestowed on Radford what became one of the wonders of Nottinghamshire. In 1780, Elliot purchased a substantial tract of land along the east bank of the River Leen – west of St Peters Street and Radford Boulevard. It was here that at great cost he built a substantial property, set on the edge of a landscaped garden. It was this park which amazed his social peers and became Elliot's legacy to the good folk of Nottingham.

Work began on the site by first excavating a large lake with a central island, which was filled by diverting part of the River Leen. Elliot had his park planted with mature trees and exotic plants, and constructed various buildings. The grounds were surrounded by a high wooden fence and entered by an ornamental wooden bridge over the river. A second equally ornate bridge crossed the lake to the island. Upon the island was a large octagonal brick tower with a pagoda-style top. The fence, buildings and bridges were all painted white.

For a few short years the public enjoyed visits to Elliot's wondrous park. It would seem that Elliot may have overstretched his finances and it is likely that

Radford Grove in its hayday. (Courtesy of the Paul Nix Collection)

as both his health and state of mind began to suffer the beauty of the place began to decline. People began to refer to the place as Elliot's F'oily or Radford Folly, and a poet penned the line: 'Famed Radford Folly left with pious haste.'

The neglect and disinterest were to continue until Elliot's death in 1792 and there matters might have ended and Radford Folly disappeared. However, newspaper magnet Mr R. Sutton purchased Elliot's entire estate and work began on reviving the folly, with plans to open it as a public pleasure ground. The lake was restocked with fish and rare birds, and the buildings and other structures had a fresh coat of white paint. The inside of the fence by the lake was painted with a mural, along with 3D cut-out buildings, representing the Bay of Naples. At night, this was illuminated with hundreds of tiny coloured oil lamps. A tea room was opened in the octagonal tower and other garden buildings adapted for the needs of the paying public.

Sutton leased the whole venture to a Mr Parr, and Elliot's Folly became known as Radford Grove – perhaps with reference to the success of Clifton Grove.

For many years the people of Nottingham enjoyed the pleasures of Radford Grove. In the summer, lavish entertainments were held with performers like the tight-rope walker 'The Great Blondin'. Fishing and boating on the lake – with rent for the boats at 1s per hour – were always popular, as were the firework displays. In short, Radford Grove became Nottingham's premier place of entertainment, of which the poet Henry Sutton wrote: 'There is a spot of earth supremely blest. A dear and sweater spot than all the rest.'

After a few years of success, the popularity of Radford Grove began to decline and Sutton decided to cut his losses. He closed the grounds to the public, had extensive alterations made to the house and once again it became a private residence. For several years Sutton and his family resided in Radford. On his death, the estate was sold to local mill owner Mr Harrison and the fame and glory of Radford Grove was overtaken by industry and grime. Harrison filled in the lake and destroyed much of the grounds. He later sold the land to the local colliery company, who were to build an engine house and coal wharf on the site. The octagonal tower remained until recent times, a sad reminder of what once was.

❧ GWYN (NELL) AND BESTWOOD LODGE ❧

Eleanor 'Nell' Gwyn (1650–1687) has been described as one of Restoration England's most celebrated actresses and more famously was the long-term mistress of Charles II. Three cities claim to be her birthplace: Hereford, London and Oxford. Of these, London, or more precisely Covent Garden, where Nell spent her childhood, is deemed to be the most likely.

Nell's father is recorded by some biographers as being of minor Welsh gentry and the son of Thomas Guine a Cap. A poem from 1681 indicates that he died in an Oxford prison. Whatever the truth, he disappears from any account of Nell's life from the time of her early childhood in Covent Garden.

To say that Nell Gwyn had an unconventional childhood is an understatement. She was raised in a London bawdy house – a brothel – run by her mother, 'Madam' or 'Old Ma Gwyn'. From an early age Nell and her notorious older sister Rose were involved in the family business. Nell, at a tender age, probably acted as a servant girl, attending the rich clients who frequented the 'house'. Even at this stage she was renowned for her beauty and quick wit.

In 1662, Nell escaped her life in the bawdy house by taking a lover, a man named Duncan or Dugan, who moved her to rooms in Maypole Ally.

During the period of the Commonwealth, theatre, along with many other entertainments, was banned. With the Restoration in 1660, Charles II quickly set about establishing new theatrical groups. In 1663, one of these, the Kings Company under Thomas Killigrew, opened a new playhouse, The Theatre in Bridge Street, later rebuilt as the Theatre Royal, Drury Lane.

It was here that Nell was to take on one of her most famous roles, that of an orange seller. A friend of Madam Gwyn's and former prostitute Mary Meggs – nicknamed 'Orange Moll' –was granted a licence by the king to 'vend, utter and sell oranges, lemons, fruit, sweetmeats and all manner of fruiterers and confectioners wares'. Nell and her sister were hired by Meggs as scantily clad 'orange-girls' selling their wares at six pence each to the theatre audience.

One of the many contemporary portraits of Nell Gwyn, mistress of Charles II.
(Author's Collection)

Nell did not remain an orange seller for long. Her beauty, quick wit and obvious talent soon brought her to the attention of the theatre company. The rest, as they say, is history and Nell became one of the most successful and popular actresses of her time. Moving now in Court circles, she came to the attention of King Charles II.

No one knows if it was love at first sight, but Nell became the king's most famous long-term mistress. The inevitable happened, and in 1670 Nell gave birth to her first son by Charles. A handsome young man, he was given the name Charles Beauclerk. A year later, in 1671, Nell gave birth to her second son, James Beauclerk.

When Charles Beauclerk was 6 years old, in 1676, the King issued a warrant granting him the 'dignities' of Baron of Heddington, county Oxford and Earl Burford in the same county. A few weeks later, James was granted the title of Lord Beauclerk.

On 5 January 1684, shortly after the death of Henry Jermyn, 1st Duke of St Albans, the King gave the title to Charles along with an allowance of £1,000 a year. Amongst the estates that the newly created duke acquired was the Royal Hunting Lodge at Bestwood in Nottinghamshire.

There are a number of legends concerning how Charles Beauclerk received his many titles and estate, and it is the local version of how he acquired Bestwood that I have chosen to retell here.

During their many years together, Charles and Nell favoured Bestwood as one of their preferred trysting places. Charles was a king who enjoyed the traditional hunt at Bestwood and he would routinely take Nell with him.

It is said that when Nell gave birth to Charles, the king refused to acknowledge him with a title and name. History tells us that this part of the story is true, for it was six years before the young Charles was given the title Baron of Heddington, co. Oxford and Earl Burford. However, the local legend states that the shrewd Nell Gwynn gained her son status by her own efforts and persistence to the king.

Eventually, frustrated with her lover's response to her pliés, she dangled the infant out of a window and told the king that she would rather the child die than see him live without a future. Charles relented and, being equally shrewd, told Nell that the boy would be granted 'all of the land Nell could ride around before breakfast'. The King was aware that Nell was seldom an early riser and believed he had set her an impossible task. However, Nell was up before dawn the very next morning and with a host of witnesses – including lawyers – she set off to ride the bounds of the Bestwood Estate.

As conformation of her course she dropped a coloured silk handkerchief on or by each of the many boundary marks. Completing the entire boundary she carefully placed the last handkerchief on the top of the Centre Stone. At breakfast she confronted the king with what she had done, stating that she had completed her part of the bargain. The astonished Charles is said to have uttered the words, 'I can't believe it! You have taken my best wood (Bestwood?).' He was forced to keep his side of the bargain and granted his son the estate and the title Duke of St Albans.

How true is this charming local story? The incident where Nell dangled the child from the window is certainly recorded as true, but not at Bestwood. Some years ago I told this story at a talk I was giving on the subject of Nottingham's

Old Stones. After the lecture I was approached by a couple whose house adjoined Bestwood Park. They informed me that at the bottom of their garden was an ancient bridle path, from which they had recovered many horse shoes. The deeds to their property recorded the story of Nell's early morning ride and went on to say that the path – the boundary between their property and Bestwood – had been established by this very act!

⁂ HIGHWAYMAN AND THE HANGMAN (THE) ⁂

This is the story of two men accused and convicted of highway robbery, highwaymen, and their executioners, the hangmen. In court records and other documents there are a number of men referred to as highwaymen; among these are John Nevison, aka Swift Nick, and Thomas Wilcox, aka Sawley Thom. These men represent the two extremes of highway robbery. However, they have two things in common; they were both labelled highwaymen after committing highway robbery and murder in Nottinghamshire, and both met their death at the end of a hangman's rope. It is also the story of their executioners, the hangmen.

The word highwayman (or woman) conjures up the rather romanticised picture of a 'Turpin'-type figure, complete with black mask and pistol, mounted on a black horse and shouting 'Stand and deliver' whilst holding up a mail coach. The truth is a little more mundane. The term highwayman was used to describe those guilty of highway robbery, any form of robbery committed on a public road or highway.

(THP)

Whilst some of these crimes were committed against mail coaches by legends like Dick Turpin and Swift Nick, the majority were opportunistic crimes committed by common criminals like Thomas Wilcox, and were what today we might term muggings. Whatever its form, highway robbery was a crime punishable by the death penalty.

A death sentence delivered by a court or judge was usually carried out by a judicial officer, appointed by the State or other legal authority. In order to protect these officials from charges of murder, they were issued with a warrant authorising or ordering them to execute the sentence – hence the term executioner. Quite often they would be called upon to administer other forms of non-lethal punishment, like floggings. Executioners, who carried out the task by hanging, were naturally known as hangmen. Like the highwayman, the hangman has its stereotypical image – that of the burly hooded or masked man. Though this may well have been the case in medieval times, by the nineteenth century executioners had become professionals who operated within their own district or county.

Case 1

Highwayman: John (William) Nevison, aka Swift Nick, was born in Wortley near Sheffield around 1639/40. Nevison is one of history's most famous and flamboyant highwaymen. Many of Nevison's exploits – including the famous ride to York – were wrongly attributed to the better-known Richard (Dick) Turpin.

Nevison is a legend, and as such his story has entered folklore with a good deal of mythos. He came from a good family and was well educated. In his school years it is reported that he was a troublemaker and prone to stealing. After leaving school he took up the profession of brewer's clerk in London. But old habits die hard and the young Nevison absconded to Holland with the money from a debt he had been sent to collect. Here he joined a regiment commanded by the Duke of York and fought with distinction in the Flanders War.

With the end of the war, Nevison retuned to York where he lived with his father. After his father's death, Nevison took to the road as a highwayman. By 1676, Nevison had already committed many crimes of highway robbery and murder and his reputation was established. One summer morning in that year, he robbed a traveller on the road at Gads Hill in Kent. Fearing that he had been recognised, Nevison made his escape and headed north. Nevison, stopping regularly for short rests, continued his journey until he arrived in York in the early evening – a distance of some 200 miles from the scene of the robbery. Realising that his incredible journey would be deemed impossible, Nevison set about establishing an alibi: he changed his clothes and mingled with a crowd who were watching a bowling match attended by the Lord Mayor. Nevison went to great pains to make certain he was noticed and even made a wager on the match with the mayor. Nevison made sure the Lord Mayor remembered the time the bet was laid – eight o'clock that evening.

After his famous ride from London to York, John Nevison's career and reputation as a highwayman continued. For a number of years Nevison and his gang of six outlaws operated out of the Talbot Inn at Newark, Nottinghamshire. From here they robbed travellers and mail coaches along the Great North Road as far north as York and as far south as Huntingdon.

He was captured and imprisoned on several occasions, but always managed to escape. In 1681 he was imprisoned in Leicester Gaol and, with the aid of accomplices, made well his escape by feigning his own death from the plague. His abilities of both escape and evading capture earned him the nickname of Swift Nick, reputedly given by Charles II, an ardent admirer of his exploits.

Inevitably, such a high-profile criminal attracted the attention of bounty hunters and after a tip-off from the landlady, Nevison was captured whilst drinking at an inn at Sandal, near Wakefield, and was taken for trial to York. Here he was found guilty of murder and highway robbery and on 4 May 1684 he was executed on the gallows at York Castle. Nevison's body was buried at St Mary's church, York, in an unmarked grave.

Executioner: The name of John Nevison's executioner is unrecorded, but the site of the execution – York's Tyburn – had a fearsome reputation. Its gallows, designed to take up to twenty-four victims at a time, consisted of a wooden triangle supported by three wooden pillars. This form of gallows was commonly known as the three-legged mare. Executions at York Castle drew large and rowdy crowds. The spectacle began with the arrival of the condemned prisoner brought to the place in a cart, sitting astride their own coffin. Until 1745, it was customary practice for the hangman to quarter the victim's body after hanging.

Scene of the crime: the junction of Derby Road and Barrack Lane. (Courtesy of the Paul Nix Collection)

Case 2

Highwayman: Thomas Wilcox, aka 'Sawley Thom'. With a nickname like Sawley Thom, one would suspect we were dealing with an illustrious felon, but this is not the case. It probably denoted the mere fact that Wilcox came from the Derbyshire village of Sawley.

Sometime in March 1820, Wilcox was said to have committed the crimes of highway robbery and murder – although some writers state there was some doubt about his guilt. He was convicted and found guilty of robbing and murdering Thomas Pearson of Chilwell, on Derby Road near Barracks Lane. Sentenced to death, Wilcox was executed on the gallows on Gallows Hill, Mansfield Road, Nottingham.

Executioner: The hanging of Thomas Wilcox at Nottingham on 29 March 1820 was the first recorded execution carried out by Leicestershire man, Samuel Haywood. Haywood was an agricultural labourer. He was also a poacher, a crime for which he was arrested in March 1817. He was tried and convicted of being found 'equipped for poaching' on Friday, 18 March 1817. Haywood was sentenced to two years' imprisonment in Leicester's Bridewell – House of Correction. Whilst imprisoned he volunteered to carry out the sentence of 'flogging' on another prisoner. Haywood must have performed his task well, because the governor offered him the vacant position of hangman for the counties of Leicestershire, Derbyshire and Nottinghamshire.

Haywood accepted the post and became a hangman, a career that was to span thirty years and led to forty-four recorded executions, with a further fourteen unconfirmed. His final execution was that of John Platts at Derby on 1 April 1847. Haywood died of influenza on 11 March 1848 at the age of 70.

❧ INSPIRATION FOR OLIVER TWIST (THE) ❧

Of the many thousands who have read Charles Dickens's *Oliver Twist*, how many know that the novel has a Nottinghamshire connection? Dickens wrote the book after reading the biography of Robert Blincoe, who was the inspiration for the title character Oliver Twist. Blincoe's life story can be counted as truly Dickensian as it contains all of the elements worthy of a Dickens' plot.

Blincoe's story begins not in Nottinghamshire but in the workhouse in St Pancras, London. Blincoe, an orphan with no recollection of his parents, had been at the institution since he was 4 years old. In August 1799, at the age of 7, Blincoe was one of eighty boys and girls of the same age, 'sold to indenture as parish apprentices' to Messers C.W. and F. Lambert of Gonalston cotton mill in the Nottinghamshire village of Lowdham. The mill was founded in 1784 by Richard Lambert on the site of a former flour mill. When the mill passed into the hands of his three sons, the Lamberts diversified into the production of fancy hosiery and lace.

The indentured apprenticeship of such young children was a common practice at this time. Children were routinely sold into apprenticeships by the workhouse overseers in private deals with mill owners, but only with the child's consent.

The St Pancras overseers knew that they could not force any of the children to take the offer of apprenticeship and so they resorted to bribery. The seven year olds were promised a better life at the mill. Here – until they were 21 – they would lead the good life, 'fed with roast beef and ride the master's horses', be well schooled and be handsomely paid to learn a trade. None of this ever happened. In effect, they were sold into slavery, ironically at a time when the government was considering abolishing slavery.

The children travelled by road to Lowdham in a convoy of covered waggons with small barred windows. The journey took five days on near starvation rations and was most uncomfortable and hot. On arrival, they found their lodgings to be no better than that of the workhouse. Whilst the boys and girls were placed into separate dormitories, they were still expected to sleep four to a bunk bed and to exist on simple meals of gruel and stale black bread. Sanitary conditions were rudimentary.

Instead of attending school the boys and girls were put straight to work in the mill. Their working day began at 5 a.m.and was between fourteen and sixteen hours a day, six days a week. Blincoe's first job was to pick up loose cotton waste from the spinning frames whilst the machines were still working. This was considered a suitable job for small children, as they were able to fit into the small spaces under the machines. This kind of work was very dangerous and accidents were frequent. Blincoe lost half a finger whilst still quite young.

Blincoe's memoirs tell how he was subjected to many beatings by the mills overlookers, who he describes as 'a set of brutal, ferocious, illiterate ruffians alike void of understanding as of humanity.' He goes on to tell how, in his first year at the mill, he contemplated suicide many times. His intention was 'to throw himself out of one of the upper windows of the factory – but when he came to look at the leap … his courage failed him.' He decided instead that he would run away and attempt to return to London. Blincoe managed to get as far as Burton Joyce when he was recognised and apprehended by a tailor, who sometimes worked at the mill. He was dragged back to Gonalston where he was beaten severely.

In 1802, Gonalston mill closed and Blincoe and the other apprentices were sent to Litton Mill, near Tideswell in Derbyshire. Here conditions were far worse than those at Gonalston. The now 10-year-old Blincoe and fellow Londoners were forced to endure appalling conditions and treatment, described as being barbaric and sadistic. Blincoe was forced to continue his apprenticeship until he was 21 and became a 'journeyman'. He continued to work at Litton as an adult operative until 1817. In that year he moved to Lancashire – the centre of the cotton trade – and opened his own small cotton spinning business. With a successful business established, in 1819 he married a woman called Martha (no surname found).

In 1822, Blincoe was interviewed by John Brown, a journalist from Bolton in Lancashire, who was writing an article on child labour. Brown was so fascinated by his experiences that he decided to write Blincoe's biography. On completion, Brown handed the document to his friend Richard Carlile, an active campaigner for factory legislation. Later that year Brown committed suicide.

Carlile went on to publish the memoirs in the radical newspaper *The Lion*. The story appeared in five weekly episodes from 25 January to 22 February 1828. Carlile also published the work in the journal *The Poor Man's Advocate*. Five years later, Robert Blincoe's memoirs were published in pamphlet form – a book which is still available to today's reader.

Even with an established and successful business, Blincoe's troubles were not over. In the very same year as his story first appeared in print, a fire destroyed his spinning machines. Unable to pay his debts, he was imprisoned in the debtors gaol in Lancaster Castle. On his release, Blincoe established himself as a cotton-waste dealer and his wife opened a small grocers shop. Once again a successful businessman, Blincoe was able to clear all his debts. Determined

Gonalston Mill, Blincoe's place of torment. (Courtesy of *The Topper*)

that his own three children would have a better future, he was able to pay for their education. One of his sons graduated from Queen's College, Cambridge, and became a Church of England clergyman.

R obert Blincoe died of bronchitis in 1860, at the home of his daughter in Gunco Lane, Macclesfield. Gonalston Mill – now a private residence – stands to this day as a testimony to the horrors of eighteenth- and nineteenth-century child labour.

❧ JACOBITES: TUXFORD AND THE REBEL STONE ❧

Tuxford and the Rebel Stone

The pretty market town of Tuxford lies alongside the 'Old' Great North Road –
(B1164) – some 21 miles north of Nottingham. Little of the original ancient
village remains, as Tuxford was almost destroyed by a great fire which broke out on
8 September 1702. The damage caused by the fire was so great that the reigning
monarch – Queen Anne – authorised a nationwide collection fund to help rebuild
the town.

Despite the fire, Tuxford has much to offer the enquiring visitor.
The twelfth-century parish church of St Nicholas contains the remains of
many of the county's noteworthy families. One such is the tomb of Thomas
de Gunthorpe, Prior of Newstead, who was buried here in 1495.

The town lock-up, built in 1823 and one of only two such remaining in the
county, must have been the height of luxury for those incarcerated within.
It contains two separate cells, each with its own 'earthcloset'. The town is lucky
enough to have a working windmill which was built in 1810 and restored in 1993,
after falling into disrepair in the 1920s.

Tuxford owes its place in history to its location on an ancient north/south
highway. The Great North Road was one of the most important roads in the
country. Tuxford's place on this ancient highway means that it had travellers from
as far away as the Scottish Highlands in the north and London in the south,
passing through its streets. For centuries, along with ordinary folk, royalty, the mail
and armies have all passed this way. It is hard to imagine now the scene in the
town when Scottish drovers passed through, with their herds of highland cattle
filling the narrow streets.

We should not think of the original Great North Road in terms of its
replacement, the modern A1, which follows much of its original route. The Old
Great North Road was nothing more than a dirt track. The land around Tuxford
over which it passes is heavy clay soil. A letter of 1640 by William Uvedale,
Treasurer at War, says: 'About Tuxford is the most absolutely ill road in the world.'
The antiquarian Throsby, travelling on horseback, describes his progress in the
district as little more than 2mph.

Delays to the mail for London prompted the authorities to publish this timetable: 'Scrooby to Tuxford – 7 miles – 2 hours. Tuxford to Newark – 10 mile, 3 hours. Newark to Grantham, – 10 miles – 1½ hours.'

Although Tuxford Nottinghamshire is clearly in the Midlands, its allegiance over 300 years ago lay with the Jacobite cause and Scotland. This fact is confirmed by a Grade II listed monument which stands to the south of the town by the western side of the Old Great North Road. This stone is around 2ft square and 6ft high and bears the inscription 'Here lyeth a rebel 1746'.

This monument, known has the Rebel Stone or Rebel's Grave, has kept a secret which, when revealed, tells us something of the attitude of the people of Tuxford nearly 300 years ago.

One clue to this secret comes in the form of the local tradition which states that the Scottish drovers, whilst passing the stone, would remove small pieces as a supposed cure for toothache. Whilst this type of 'folk cure' is not uncommon, in this case were the drovers using it as a cover story in order to pay homage to a fallen clansman or even a local sympathiser?

The Rebel Stone, or Rebel's Grave, became a listed monument in 1985. The listing document describes it as 'A mid-eighteenth century Ashlar 2m high with a splayed base and moulded cap. The stone is said to mark the burial place of a Scotsman who fell in the rebellion of 1745/46'.

Who was this Scottish rebel and why was he buried so far from home? The statement on the listing document implies that he was a Jacobite – derived from Jacobus, the Latin word for James. Jacobite was the name given to supporters of James Stuart. Before the Act of Union in 1707, James was crowned James II of England, King of Ireland and James VII of Scotland in 1685. His Catholic faith and pro-French persuasion was seen as unsuitable for an English monarch and he was deposed by Parliament in the Glorious Revolution of 1688. His eldest daughter, Mary, and her Dutch-born husband, Prince William of Orange – both of whom were Protestants – were invited to take the throne and were jointly crowned in 1689.

These events triggered the Jacobite Risings, which began as a political movement seeking the restoration of the Stuart dynasty. James's Scottish origin meant that much of his support came from the north. However, Jacobite clubs and societies held secret meeting in towns and cities throughout the country. In an attempt to place James's son, Charles Edward Stuart (Bonnie Prince Charlie), on the throne, two bouts of armed insurrection – known as 15th and 45th Rebellion – took place in 1715 and 1745. The Jacobite Rebellion finally ended in 1746 after the defeat of Charles' army at the Battle of Culloden in 1745.

Local legend says that a group of Jacobite rebels were being transported south to face trial and possible execution in London. Just south of Tuxford, one

The Rebel Stone, standing by the old road to the north. (Courtesy of the Paul Nix Collection)

of these men attempted an escape. Rolling or jumping from the back of the cart in which he was travelling, he hit the ground with such force as to break his neck and die.

Someone amongst the crowd of locals following the prisoners and escort organised a rudimentary military funeral, and he was buried close to the spot where he died. The town drum was hired to sound the retreat as the man was lowered to his grave. Sometime later, a substantial monument was erected on the site.

Closer examination of the story finds that it does not quite fit with fact. Directly after the Battle of Culloden, many of the prisoners taken in the field were summarily executed on the spot. Many hundreds were taken prisoner in the following year. Whilst the leaders of the rebellion were brought to trial in London, the rest were sold into seven years of servitude to the American Colonists. In the beginning, most were shipped direct from Scottish ports, but as numbers grew a fleet of transport ships took the prisoners south to be held at places like Tilbury Fort, there to await transportation to America.

A mystery has always surrounded the monument. Why would someone pay for an expensive memorial to an unknown Scottish rebel? The answer might lie in the 1695 diary of the clergyman Oliver Heywood. In September of that year he wrote that he had witnessed the spirits of Papists and Jacobites at work in Nottinghamshire. Perhaps he was referring to Tuxford, where we find that meetings of Non-Jurats and Jacobites were regularly held at the house of the postmaster?

✤ KING'S GRAVE (A): ✤
THE GRAVE OF THE GYPSY KING

On the north side of St Helen's churchyard, Selston, is a memorial said to mark the grave of a Gypsy King. The stone simply reads: 'The Grave of Dan Boswell Gipsy King 1737–1827'. Followed by: 'I've lodged in many a town / I've travelled many a year. / But death at length has brought me down, to my last lodging here.'

The stone is not the original and it also records Boswell's birth inaccurately. In 1906 the original stone is described as being broken and only partly legible, with no verse inscribed upon it. The parish burial register records that Daniel Boswell was buried on 2 March 1827 at the age of 76 and not 90 as the stone claims, making the year of his birth 1751.

So, who was Dan Boswell and how did he come to be buried in the churchyard of this north Nottinghamshire village?

We must not assume that the title of king (or queen) in the Gypsy context bears any relationship to the use of the word in a conventional sense. Gypsies or travellers by their very nature are a nomadic people with strong family and clan loyalties. Male elders and chieftains were often honoured with the title of 'King' and their wives Queen.

The grave of the Gipsy King at Selston and the Boswell family name in connection with the title are not unique. There are many graves scattered throughout Britain which purport to be those of Gypsy royalty and the name Boswell appears on more than one of them.

The Boswells, an extended family of travellers, were for centuries one of the largest and most powerful of the Gypsy clans. They were frequently seen throughout the county, to the extent that the old Nottinghamshire dialect word 'bos'll' – deriving from Boswell – was used as a term for travellers and Roma in general. Selston Common was a frequent stopover site.

In 1835, another member of the Boswell clan, Louis Boswell, died in the vicinity of Bestwood and was buried in Eastwood churchyard. The burial register describes him as a 'Traveller aged 42'. There is a marginal note which says, 'This man known as the king of the Gypsies was interred in the presence of a vast concourse of spectators'.

Dan Boswell's grave at Selston churchyard. (Courtesy of the Paul Nix Collection)

Another Boswell with Nottinghamshire connections, James Boswell, who died on 30 January 1708, is buried in Rossington near Doncaster, Yorkshire. The *Topographical Dictionary of Yorkshire* (1822), records that his headstone bore the inscription 'James Bosvill [*sic*], King of the Gypsies'. Legend has it that James lived in Sherwood Forest and would help the needy, both Gypsies and non-Gypsies alike. A few months after his death, James Boswell's grave was opened so that his cat might be buried by his side. This incident is said to have given rise to the appearance of a ghostly cat which is frequently to be seen sitting on the churchyard wall by the grave.

Whatever the extent of the Gypsy Kings' earthly power, their influence seems to have extended beyond the grave. For a number of years it was the custom of Gypsies from the south to make an annual visit to the grave of James Boswell. Part of this custom was to pour a flagon of ale over the grave. This seems to have been a common mark of respect and was also a custom associated with the graves of other Gypsy Kings, including that of Louis Boswell at Eastwood.

It is not recorded that the ale-pouring custom was ever performed over the grave of Dan Boswell. However, it was traditional for Gypsies to lay newborn babies on Dan's grave in order to bring them future good luck.

❧ LABYRINTH: THE SHEPHERD'S RACE ❧

'The nine-men's morris is filled up with mud. And the quaint mazes
on the wanton green for lack of tread are undistinguishable'

William Shakespeare

Perhaps the most curious and least understood ancient monument in Nottingham
is the turf maze known as the Shepherd's Race or Robin Hood's Race. The maze
has long since disappeared, but the debate over its origin and use continues.

Turf mazes are created by cutting a serpentine path into a level area of open
grass. Commonly the path of the maze is or was created from the turfed area
between narrow channels of bare earth. In a few instances the path is defined by
the channel itself; the latter is the case with the Shepherd's Race.

The design or pattern of mazes falls into two distinct groups, known as classical
(Cretan) and medieval. Many European examples are of the classical design, whilst
those in England are mainly medieval.

Although generically referred to as mazes, strictly speaking they should be
called labyrinths. A maze is a puzzle with numerous paths and dead ends whilst a
labyrinth is a single path leading to a centre point and back out.

The purpose of the maze seems to have been to run, dance or walk the path to
the centre and back out – possibly without a pause. This was known as 'treading
the maze' and was a popular event at village fairs and other festivals. There is
evidence indicating that in some of the larger mazes 'treading' may have been a
processional event.

Mazes are historically confined to Northern Europe, including England, Wales,
Germany, Denmark, Lapland, Iceland and parts of the former Soviet Union
including the Czech Republic and Poland. Hundreds of examples still exist in
Scandinavia, where the paths are marked out using stones.

Shakespeare's lines quoted above suggest that the maze was once a common
sight in the sixteenth-century English landscape. There are now only eight
examples of turf mazes in existence. However, there are – including two in
Nottinghamshire – references to over twenty extinct examples. None of these
appear restricted to any particular geographical location. Whilst there are no

The Shepherd's Race. Deering's original plan. (Author's Collection)

recorded examples of the mazes in Ireland, the maze design is found calved into a granite boulder known as the Hollywood Stone, in County Wicklow. The carving has been dated at around AD 550. However, this date is probably pure conjecture.

English mazes are usually circular in design and between 30ft and 60ft in diameter, although square and polygonal examples are known. They appear to have been commonly located on village greens and commons, often close to a church or chapel. Other examples are known in more remote spots, by crossroads and on hill tops. There are few references to turf mazes earlier than the late seventeenth century, and a number of existing examples are claimed to have been cut at this time.

Returning to the quote from Shakespeare's *A Midsummers Night's Dream*, for the reference to the maze to have had any impact with the audience, turf mazes must have been a familiar sight. However, if the words are to be taken literally, by the late sixteenth century mazes may have been in decline for lack of use; 'The quaint mazes on the wanton green for lack of tread are undistinguishable.'

By their very nature, turf mazes are ephemeral and need constant maintenance to uphold their existence. Such maintenance destroys possible archaeological evidence for dating their original creation. References to the cutting of a 'new' maze in the sixteenth/seventeenth century may indicate the re-cutting of a maze which had become overgrown and forgotten

There are no records as to when the Shepherd's Race was cut into the flat ground near the summit of Blue Bell Hill (Thornywood Mount) in the St Ann's district of Nottingham. The hill was formerly part of Sneinton Common, given to the parish as common land by the Pierpont family.

It is described as being 34–35 yards across, covering an area of 324 square yards, with a single path 535 yards long. These proportions make the Shepherd's Race one of the largest examples of its kind. Its design is fairly typical of the medieval kind – with the addition of four rounded extensions or bastions. Each enclosed a small mound with a design, known in heraldry as a 'cross-crosslet', cut into the top. The bastions are said to have aligned with the four cardinal points of the compass. This feature is not unique to the Shepherd's Race, as the existing maze at Saffron Walden in Essex also has bastions, though without the additional cross-crosslets.

The name Shepherd's Race is not confined to the Nottingham maze. The now lost maze on the village green at Boughton Green in Northamptonshire was known as Shepherd Ring or Shepherd's Race. The use of the word shepherd in the title is thought to have derived from the once widely held belief that mazes were cut by shepherds as a sort of exercise ground.

Had the Shepherd's Race at St Ann's in Nottingham survived, without doubt it would have been one of the finest examples of its kind. It is strange, then, that it has always been a footnote in history, an appendix to notes on the more famous St Ann's Well.

Because of their close proximity – around 300 yards – the Shepherd's Race and famous St Ann's Well have always been considered as part of a single ritual site. However, there is little actual evidence for this being the case. This speculative link was re-enforced by the fact that at least two nineteenth-century copies of the maze were created close to the well, though neither were full size. The smaller of the two was close to the well, whilst the larger was created in a tea garden not far from the original maze site not long after it had been destroyed. It is this replica which fooled the Ordnance Survey team, making an appearance as 'The Shepherd's Race' on the 1836 map. It does not make an appearance on subsequent editions.

As with most mazes, the origin of the Shepherd's Race is speculative. One modern author on the subject states that the maze was cut in the fourth century and modified later by the Knights Templar for use in their rituals. Two eighteenth-century antiquarians pass comment on the maze. William Stukeley, the father of archaeology, delivers a popular opinion of the time when he declares it to be 'of Roman origin'. Charles Deering says, 'It seems to be a name of no old standing.' He disputes Stukeley's opinion and declares: 'It is evidently, from the cross-crosslets in the centres of the four lesser rounds; and in that there are no banks raised but circular trenches cut into the turf, and those so narrow that persons cannot run in them, but must run on top of the turf, it is of no Roman origin, and yet is more ancient than the reformation.'

Although a wonderful description of the maze, Deering is contradicted by contemporary plans which clearly show the path to be the bare earth between the turf walls. He was of the opinion that it was cut by the monks of the nearby Chapel of St Ann for the purpose of exercise and meditation. At least one Victorian writer – Bishop Edward Trollope – agreed with Deering and produced a charming, if inaccurate, illustration of kneeling monks on the turf path of the maze.

The origin of the Shepherd's Race may be in dispute; however, its demise is not. Following the Enclosure Act, the maze was ploughed up and the area planted with potatoes on 17 February 1797.

By the time this book is in circulation, the Shepherd's Races, or at least an acknowledgement to the original, will once again be a Nottinghamshire curiosity! A new version is in the final stages of construction, close to the Visitors Centre of the St Ann's Allotments. This mini replica follows closely the design of the original Shepherd's Race and is intended to be a tribute rather than a replica. The new attraction will be open to the public and will allow visitors to once again 'tread the maze'.

⁑ LEEDS MAIL (THE) ⁑

The A60 Mansfield Road developed from a prehistoric trackway, an ancient north–south link running through the heart of Sherwood Forest. For many centuries it remained a sandy ill-defined track, deeply rutted with the passage of carts and waggons pulled by teams of oxen or horses. It was not until 1787 and the passing of the 'Mansfield Turnpike Act' that the condition of the road began to improve.

In the late eighteenth, early nineteenth centuries, a familiar sight along the Mansfield Road was the Leeds Mail. Four- and six-horse coaches with names like The Champion, The Royal Hope, The Old Robin Hood, The Express, The Brilliant, and The Rapid, departed from Nottingham for Leeds, twice daily at 6 a.m. and 6 p.m.

It was not just the state of the road which made the route difficult to travel. Bad weather, particularly snow, made matters worse. On Friday, 8 April 1709 the snow was so deep that the coach was unable to leave Nottingham and the mail was sent on by horse-back rider.

The number of coaches travelling along the road meant that it was necessary to stable horses at regular intervals along the route to enable a change of team and rest tired horses.

The 11 February 1772 was a bitterly cold day and the snow lay thick on the ground. Two men, Thomas Rhodes and John Curtis, were leading a team of six horses back to Mansfield. At a point on the road somewhere around The Hutt, one of the men spotted a splash of scarlet against the white snow. This proved to be the jacket of a half-frozen soldier lying in a deep snowdrift.

Rhodes and Curtis managed to revive the man, unharnessed a horse, set him upon it and, slapping its flank, set it galloping off towards Mansfield. But the two Samaritans had committed a fatal error. They had unwittingly set the man on the lead horse of the team and with their leader gone the rest proved difficult to handle.

The soldier arrived safely in Mansfield and after making a full recovery managed to tell his tale. However, his rescuers, Rhodes and Curtis, managed to struggle on a matter of a few hundred yards before collapsing. Both were later found frozen to death on the spot where they had fallen. One left a widow and eight children.

Even by the early 1800s the weather could still prevent the mail from getting through. On Friday, 28 January 1814 the Leeds Mail left Nottingham at its usual time of 6 p.m. By 9.30 p.m. the snow was so deep that it had travelled barely 8 miles. At a point just past Seven Mile House, the outside passengers were about to go inside for the night when one of their number spotted a man lying by the road. It proved to be 70-year-old man called Allison. He had walked from Mansfield that morning and, returning home, was overcome by the storm. Allison was revived by the passengers, but the coach was now axel deep in snow. Allison and his rescuers spent the night at a nearby farm, whilst the coach was forced to return to Nottingham.

$\mathcal{M}$

⁂ MAIDS ⁂

The Fair Maid of Clifton

The story of the Fair Maid of Clifton bears all the hallmarks of an ancient legend. There are many versions of the story, but I will tell it here in its most simplest of forms, as it has always been told by the folk of Clifton – a true folk story.

Long ago at Clifton there dwelt a young milkmaid. Margaret was her name. Some say that she was the fairest maid in the entire county, others that she was the fairest in the land. Many a lad sought to court her and win her hand, but she refused them all. Each day she would take the milk from her father's cows to Wilford, where she would cross the river to sell it at the market in Nottingham. The ferryman was a handsome young man by the name of Bateman. Very soon, after many trips back and forth across the river, the young couple fell madly in love. Every spare moment they spent together. Each evening, when Margaret retuned from the market, Bateman would walk her home. Hand in hand they would go, along Clifton's famous Grove. They became the talk of the village, Margaret and her Bateman.

Every man was jealous, but none more so than German, a wealthy widower who had desired the beautiful girl since his wife had died. Then came the day that broke young Bateman's heart. His lord and master was going away to some far foreign land and needed his services. That evening, as the two lovers walked along the wooded path, his heart was heavy with the news he must tell his dear one. As if in sympathy, the summer air was heavy too, with distant rolls of thunder. Margaret knew there was something wrong that night but dared not break the silence between them.

When they reached the highest point along the Grove, they stopped beneath the trees and Bateman took her in his arms. A distant church clock chimed the hour of midnight and a roll of thunder echoed the last chime. Bateman gazed into Margaret's eyes and with faltering words broke his news. Margaret choked back her tears as another roll of thunder ripped the sky. Bateman took the gold ring from his finger and cut it in two. Half he gave to his love, and the other he placed in his pocket. Together they plighted their troth. Margaret would wait for Bateman's return and then they would be married in the village church at the end of the Grove.

The two thought that their words together that night had been heard by only God himself. But they were wrong. A grey-haired old woman had stood close by, unseen by the lovers. She was the village 'wise woman', the midwife who had delivered most of the young folk of Clifton, including Margaret. Some called her a witch, but she called herself the guardian of the Grove, this sacred place of lovers. She was pleased with what she had heard, for she had kept an eye on the fair Margaret all her life, and thought Bateman a suitable match.

It was a sad day when Bateman departed and Margaret was only consoled by the fact that when he returned they would be married. Among the throng of villagers that watched him go were two who had their own thoughts; the grey-haired old woman looked forward to the happy day of the wedding, but German looked on with envious eyes. Now he could make his move. The very next day German went to see Margaret's father and asked for her hand in marriage. He was not a particularly wealthy man, just an average tenant farmer. He had not much approved of his daughter's choice for a husband, Bateman the lowly ferryman. Now he saw his chance. If he could persuade Margaret to marry the wealthy German, he and his wife could have a happy life in their retirement.

Each day, for a whole week, German called at the little farmhouse and every time Margaret would refuse to see him and each time her father and mother would rebuke her. Finely, on the Sunday, she relented and agreed to marry German. The very next week the couple was married and the entire village rejoiced, except for the grey-haired old woman who would not enter the church.

For a year and a day young Bateman had been away and now he walked along the Grove to his beloved Margaret's home. Clutching his half of the gold ring and with joy in his heart he strode up to the door. But from her parents he heard the news that Margaret had married German and not only this, but she was 'with child'. Some say that the brokenhearted Bateman hanged himself at the door of his feckless lover, but I will tell you a different tale. Bateman returned along the Grove, his mind in turmoil. When he reached the highest point above the river, the very spot where he had plighted his troth, he chanced to meet with German coming the other way. The two began to argue and then to wrestle. They fought and wrestled for a whole day but neither could best the other. Finely, the ground beneath their feet gave way and the two plunged into the foaming Trent. Watching the fight was the grey-haired old woman, who returned to the village to report the events. An immediate search of the river below the Grove was made, but of the two protagonists, only Bateman's hat and German's shoe were ever found.

When Margaret heard the news her heart was full of fear. She knew that by breaking her oath to Bateman, she had caused the deaths and God would punish her. She knew too that God's justice would not be meted out whilst the innocent babe was in her belly. Where other women looked forward to the birth of their child with joy, Margaret lived in mortal fear. When the time for her confinement came, her friend and relatives took her to the village church. Here, they locked and barricaded the doors. While Margaret's mother and the midwife prepared for the birth, the rest, along with the minister, prayed for the poor girl's soul.

The night was a stormy one and thunder and lightning were in the air. The innocent babe was born safely just before the hour of midnight. The little congregation were so tired from their night of fervent prayer that they all fell into a deep sleep. Their sleep was a short one; a sudden loud clap of thunder shook the church. All awoke, except the newborn babe who slept the sleep of the innocent in his grandmother's arms. To their surprise Margaret was gone, but the doors were still locked and barred. Out into the night they rushed, headlong into the wild storm. Soon, they reached the highest point of the Grove. There stood Margaret on the very spot where she had made her promise and from which Bateman and German had plunged to their deaths. Now, above the wind's howl, they heard the clock begin to strike the hour of midnight. As they watched, from out of the dark skies two frightful demons appeared. Swooping down, they seized Margaret by the arms and carried her aloft. On the last stroke of the hour, down they plunged into the foaming waters below. That was the last that anyone was to see of Margaret, the feckless Fair Maid of Clifton. What happened to her child? The tale does not say.

The Maid of Broxtowe

As well as the legendary Fair Maid of Clifton, Nottingham has a second fair maid. She is Agnes Willoughby, the Maid of Broxtowe. Unlike her Clifton counterpart, Agnes' story is supposedly based on actual events. Writer Thomas Bailey, in his book *Annals of Nottinghamshire*, gives Agnes the title Maid of Broxtowe. In fact, Bailey is wrong; she should really be called the Maid of Aspley and, perhaps, Nottingham's own Juliet. Her story is set amidst the turbulent times of the English Civil War and is the tale of two houses, Broxtowe Hall and Aspley Hall.

The dwelling known as Broxtowe Hall stood on the site of the ancient manor of Broculeston. Passing through various hands, it was never more than a large country house. It was demolished in 1937 with the building of the Broxtowe estate, to make way for the houses on Broxtowe Hall Close (off Broxtowe Lane). Although the site at Aspley is not as ancient as Broxtowe, the house has a more interesting history. More correctly know as Aspley Woodhouse, the area was an ancient forest that stretched into Wollaton and Bilborough. The first house on the site was a hunting lodge belonging to Lenton Priory (a sort of country retreat for the prior and his important guests). This building was a tower house, a stone tower with a wooden hall and kitchen attached. After the Dissolution, the lodge become the property of the Blyth family along with the valuable rights to timber and grazing. By 1600 the house had passed into the hands of a branch of the Willoughby family and was greatly remodelled. The tower remained a feature until the house was demolished in 1968. Aspley Hall was located a few hundred yards along Robin's Wood Road from its junction with Aspley Lane.

During the Civil War, Broxtowe Hall was fortified and held for Parliament under the command of a dashing young puritan officer, Captain Thornhaugh. Aspley Hall, on the other hand, had been fortified for the king by the devoutly Catholic Willoughby family. It is said that the two opposing sides eyed each other with a mutual contempt that seldom came to blows. This, however, is not quite true, as both properties were damaged during the conflict.

Agnes Willoughby was a very beautiful and pious young lady known for her acts of charity and other Christian works. One Sunday morning in 1645, Agnes set out from Aspley to take alms to a poor family who lived close by the church in Bilborough. Later that day, her mission complete, Agnes set out to return home. At the same time, unbeknown to Agnes, Thornhaugh had set out, clutching his bible in hand, on his usual contemplative walks, and was heading in the direction of Bilborough. A little way out of the village, Agnes was set upon by three armed rouges. Her screams came to the attention of Thornhaugh, who by this time was close by. He drew his pistol and ran in the direction of the cries. By the time he reached the spot of the affray, Agnes had already been dragged from her horse and the men were about to violate her. Thornhaugh shouted a warning and shot dead one of the men. Not eager to tangle the gallant captain, the other two fled. Thornhaugh comforted the frightened girl and at great risk to himself escorted her home to her grateful father. From that moment there was an instant attraction between the two young people. Thornhaugh, under a flag of truce, returned regularly to Aspley Hall to enquire as to Agnes's health. When duties prevented such visits, Thornhaugh would write a long letter expressing his concerns for her wellbeing. Clearly both were in love. It was a love that could not be. The two were not only on opposite sides in a bloody conflict, their political and religious views were diametrically opposed. Agnes prayed for her love's soul and begged him to renounce his heretical beliefs. Thornhaugh for his part was a good and loyal soldier and Puritan to the roots. Despite his aching heart he could not give these things up. Then, one cold November morning, Thornaugh received orders from his commander, Colonel Hutchinson: the captain was to take his small force and join the siege of Shelford. This he dutifully did, but whilst engaged in the action he was shot through the chest and mortally wounded. When she heard of his death, Agnes was inconsolable. She took to eating simple foods, dressing plainly and resolved never to marry. Agnes lived for another sixty years and dedicated that time to good works, praying for the soul of her love and believing that God would see fit to unite them in the afterlife.

❧ MANSFIELD ROAD (THE) ❧

The Nottingham to Mansfield Road – A60, Mansfield Road – is considered to be one of the oldest continuously used roads in the county. From leaving Nottingham's medieval town gate, the old road was around 25 miles long, almost due north through the wilds of what was once Sherwood Forest, to the centre of the forest town of Mansfield. It was once a part of an ancient route connecting London to York. We must not imagine this as a super highway, like the modern M1, but rather a series of linked, ancient, prehistoric trackways, which eventually developed into roads.

The importance of the Mansfield Road is confirmed by the fact that it is recorded in the Domesday Book of 1068. Here it is referred to as 'the road towards York' and is declared as being a 'King's Highway'. Such roads were governed by Royal Decree, with their own laws, one of which forbade 'the ploughing or the making of a ditch within two perches of the road (33ft) on pain of a fine of £8' – around £5,000 in today's money. The compliance of this law meant that all of the early settlements within the forest – such as Arnold, now a city suburb – were built well back from the road, with their own connecting tracks.

Before the advent of the turnpike road in the eighteenth century, the Mansfield Road remained a sandy ill-defined track, deeply rutted with the passage of carts and waggons pulled by teams of oxen or horses. Maintenance of the road was patchy and was carried out at the expense of the local landowners.

From Nottingham, the old Mansfield Road followed much of the route it does today, except in the district of Ravenshead, where until 1785 it passed via Papplewick, through the grounds of Newstead Abbey rejoining the modern road just past Larch Farm.

Long before the advent of the signpost and even regular milestones to aid the travellers navigation through Sherwood Forest, the road was marked at intervals by stones known as the Great Guide Stones. The name and location of three of these stones still survive today. By chance they happen to be stones that mark the beginning, middle and end of the route between Nottingham and Mansfield. At the Nottingham end was the White Stone. This was on the eastern side of the road at the top of Gallows Hill, around where St Andrew's church now stands. Approximately halfway to Mansfield, the Robin Hood's Stone does not make an appearance in any historical reference and only features on Ogilby's Map (1675). It is shown as a tall pillar on the western side of the old road just south of its junction with a track to the village of Blidworth. This would now equate with a spot somewhere around the main gates to Newstead Abbey. The third stone, known as the John Martyn Stone, stood outside Ye Lether Bottell public house, at the corner of the Mansfield Road and Forest Lane, formerly Bottle Lane in Mansfield. The stone received its name because of an inscription on the Mansfield side which was purportedly made by a former landlord of the pub. The inscription read: 'John Martyn Stone I am, shows ye great road to Nottingham. 1621.' The stone was broken up after the death of a local postman.

A document relating to a 'Perambulation of Sherwood Forest' made in 1218 by the Knights and Free Tenants of Nottingham, provides a good description of the route. The precession is recorded as starting on Trent Bridge and proceeding through the town via Stanstrate – Stoney Street. The road exited through the north gate of the town walls, around the modern entrance to the Victoria Shopping Centre. It then climbed Gallows Hill to the lost village of Hwitstan (Whitestone), close to the junction of Mansfield Road and Mapperley Road. This purposely built village, complete with its own chapel dedicated to St Michael, was the home of the Foresters, the official woodsmen who looked after the Royal Forests and administered forest law in Sherwood. Here too was the first of the Guide Stones, the White Stone, from which the village takes its name.

The next part of the route, through what is now Arnold, is recorded as being over Red Hill, via the *rubeam rodam* – red road. Red Hill did not have the modern cutting through it and presented a considerable obstacle. Because of the state of the road from this point on, it was considered necessary for those uncertain of the route to take a guide. For this purpose the 'Guide House' was built on the Nottingham side of the hill. Here, the traveller could obtain the services of a guide to continue their journey.

Having passed over Red Hill, the road continues north into the remoteness of the forest. For any traveller before the end of the seventeenth century the next landmark on the road would have been the Robin Hood's Stone. Close by this stone there was a building which would have been of great comfort to our hypothetical traveller, The Hutt.

The Hutt was built sometime in the twelfth century as a garrison for men-at-arms to guard the highway through the forest. It was one of seven such huts built in the seven Royal Forests. It became a gathering point for solitary travellers to wait until there were sufficient numbers, before continuing their journey together through the notorious and aptly named 'Thieves Wood'.

If our traveller avoided or survived any encounter with thieves, vagabonds, outlaws and highwaymen they would eventually reach the outskirts of Mansfield and doubtlessly regard the sight of the John Martyn Stone as a welcoming one.

By the seventeenth century, the state of British roads prompted the introduction of Turnpike Trusts. These were bodies set up by individual Acts of Parliament to maintain principal roads by the application of tolls. This was the beginning of the gated toll roads known as turnpikes. However, turnpikes did not begin to make much of a difference until the eighteenth century.

In 1785, Mr Palmer of Bath, a mail coach proprietor, was trying to speed up the mail between London and Leeds. However, the Nottingham to Mansfield part of the route proved to be problematic due to the poor state of the road. Palmer's efforts resulted in the passing of the Mansfield Turnpike Act in 1787.

Despite its continued poor state of repair, the Mansfield Road in the 1700s was a busy highway. The ancient building known as the Hutt had become a coaching inn, and there were a great number of taverns, inns and ale houses on the once lonely section of road through Arnold to Red Hill.

As the road improved, regular milestones were introduced along the route. A group of cottages grew up around the stone which marked the 7-mile point. One of these became known as Seven Mile House and for many years provided refreshments in the form of cups of tea and gingerbread to the weary traveller.

The A60, Mansfield Road continues to be a well-used and much travelled road between Nottingham and Mansfield, but how many of those who ply its route know of its ancient origin and long history? As well as playing a pivotal role in the history of travel and communication in Nottinghamshire, the Mansfield Road is at the heart of many of the stories in this book.

❧ MARTYRS OF THE REFORMATION ❧ AND THE FIRST SAINTS

'Lo, dost thou not see Meg, that these blessed fathers be now as cheerfully going to their deaths as bridegrooms to their marriage?'

Thomas More

In 1531, Beauvale Priory, the little Charterhouse in the beautiful valley, received a new prior. He was a 44-year-old Essex man called John Houghton (St John Houghton) who had been sent to Beauvale by the main Carthusian House in London. John was educated at Cambridge where he graduated with degrees in civil and Canon law around 1506. Despite his parents' wishes, he entered the ministry and was ordained a parish priest. John served as a priest for four years, before he felt drawn to the Carthusian Order. He entered the London novitiate of the Order and was professed around the year 1516. He was later to serve in the role of sacristan – responsible for the contents of the church, especially the sacristy – and continued in this office until becoming Prior of Beauvale.

John remained at Beauvale for only six months before he was called back to become the prior of the London Charterhouse. John's short time at Beauvale in 1531 must have been a happy one for the monks. He is known for being a self-disciplined holy man, with a firm but sensible handling of those serving under him.

Little is known about the early life of John's successor, Robert Lawrence (St Robert Lawrence). It is believed that he may have been born in Dorset and served as chaplain to the Duke of Norfolk before becoming a monk at the London Charterhouse. Given the facts, it is likely that John Houghton and Robert Lawrence knew each other well and that it was Houghton who recommended the posting of

Lawrence to Beauvale. Whatever the circumstances, Beauvale had drawn two men together and would link them forever in history to events that were to change the English Church forever and bring about their deaths as martyrs to their cause.

King Henry VIII had grown increasingly frustrated by the fact that his wife, Catherine of Aragon, had failed to produce an heir to the throne. In 1526, Henry began his pursuit of Anne Boleyn and began the process of seeking an annulment of his marriage from Pope Clement VII. When Clement refused the annulment, Henry took matters into his own hands and had Thomas Cranmer, Archbishop of York, declare his marriage to Catherine null and void, before marrying Anne. Henry was subsequently excommunicated by the Pope and the stage was now set for Prior John and Prior Robert to play their part in history.

In 1533, in order to make any issue of his marriage to Anne legitimate, Henry had Parliament pass the First Act of Succession. This Act made the then unborn Princess Elizabeth (Henry was expecting Anne's first child would be a son), the true successor to the Crown and declared his daughter by Catherine, Mary, a 'bastard'. The Act also required that all subjects, if commanded, swear an oath of recognition and the king's supremacy in the matter. Refusal to take the oath was considered an act of treason.

Treason was a crime considered worthy of the most terrible form of execution and the condemned were sentenced to be 'hung, drawn and quartered'. The victim was first drawn to the scaffold on a wooden hurdle, where they were then partially hung on a gallows without a drop, and cut down whilst still conscious. Placed on a table or bench their private parts were cut off and their bowels, entrails and heart removed before their eyes. The body was then decapitated and cut into quarters, which were all displayed as a warning to others not to commit the same crime.

Prior John Houghton and some of the monks at the London Charterhouse refused to acknowledge the Act of Succession and were detained in the Tower of London. After a month, John agreed to sign the oath, 'As far as the law of Christ allows'. John, as a qualified lawyer, knew that this option would not be acceptable and he had only bought a little time for himself.

By February 1535, matters moved on apace, as Henry quickly moved to establish control of the situation. Parliament closed this loophole of conscious in the law and declared that everyone, particularly the clergy, had to take the Oath of Supremacy which declared Henry Supreme Head of the Church of England.

Prior Robert Lawrence of Beauvale and Prior Augustine Webster of the Charterhouse at Axholme in Lincolnshire travelled to London to discuss the issue with Prior John Houghton. This brought all three of the Carthusian Charterhouses together. After three days of prayer they contacted the king's chief commissioner Thomas Cromwell to seek for themselves and the monks under them exemption from taking the oath. This was instantly refused and the three priors were thrown into the Tower of London, accused of treason.

The King or Cromwell intended to make examples of the three Churchmen and they were brought to trial in April 1535. At first the jury were reluctant to convict, but powerful arguments from Cromwell changed their minds. They were found guilty and sentenced to be executed at Tyburn on 4 May 1535. On the morning of their execution the three priors were allowed to go to their deaths wearing their vestments, instead of the usual humiliation of being stripped naked.

Prior of Beauvale: St John Houghton. (Author's Illustration)

Thomas More, himself imprisoned in the Tower on charges of treason for refusing to sign the oath, watched them depart and commented to his daughter, 'Lo, dost thou not see Meg, that these blessed fathers be now as cheerfully going to their deaths as bridegrooms to their marriage?'

Having been tied to hurdles and dragged through the streets to Tyburn, they reached their place of execution. John Houghton was the first on the scaffold. He was offered a pardon if he denied the Pope's authority, which he refused. He addressed the crowd, forgave his executioner and requested time to pray. Having recited the first six verses of Psalm 30, he was hanged and cut down while semi-conscious. His last words as his entrails were torn out were, 'O most holy Jesus, have mercy on me in this hour', and as his heart was removed, 'Good Jesu, what will you do with my heart?' His body was then decapitated and quartered and the parts plunged in a cauldron of burning pitch to preserve them to be displayed as a warning to others. Prior Robert Lawrence and Prior Augustine Webster suffered the same fate, meeting their end with equal bravery.

On 25 October 1970, John Houghton and Robert Lawrence, Priors of Beauvale, were canonized by the Catholic Church and declared Pro-martyrs (first martyrs) of the English Reformation. St John Houghton and St Robert Lawrence's feast days are observed on 4 May, the anniversary of their martyrdom.

In 1978 the Beauvale Society was formed by Mrs L. Millar and her daughter to 'venerate the martyrs St John Houghton and St Robert Lawrence and spread knowledge and devotion to them'. In late 2006 the Society commissioned a memorial stone, carved by a local stonemason. The stone, weighing 4.4 tons and standing over 7ft tall, was erected on the site of the high altar of the Priory church, on 26 January 1978.

The ruins of the little priory and charterhouse at Beauvale has now become a place of pilgrimage for those wishing to venerate the two saints or visitors curious to see this Nottinghamshire ruin, which played its part in the history of our nation.

⚜ MINING DISASTER ⚜

In these days when health and safety seems to permeate every level of our lives, it is hard to imagine a time when a badly nailed plank of wood could lead to the death of fourteen men. However, this was the case in 1913 at the Bolsover Colliery Company's new workings at Rufford, 5 miles north-east of Mansfield, Nottinghamshire.

In 1911, the Bolsover Colliery Company had acquired the right to mine coal, mainly under 5,000 acres of Lord Savile's land. They were seeking to exploit the highly lucrative top-hard seam, which here lies at around the depth of 554 yards.

Using a steam crane, work on the new colliery began by sinking two shafts – No. 1 at 21ft in diameter and No. 2 at 18ft in diameter. Cutting down through the native sandstone, No. 1 shaft had reached a depth of 80ft when water was encountered and work stopped. It was decided at this point to erect permanent headgear, with winding engines and winding houses. By 5 June 1912, the erecting and installing of plant and machinery was complete and work resumed on sinking the shafts. Water was still a problem, but could now be effectively dealt with by a method known as tubbing – lining the shaft with wooden planks enforced with metal hoops.

At the end of 1912, No. 1 shaft had reached a depth of 145 yards and the bottom of the sandstone. The next rock strata encountered was magnesium limestone. It was anticipated that this layer would be dry, but cutting through the strata a further 12 yards water was once again encountered. Sinking was continued for a few more yards – to around a total depth of 162 yards – when it was decided that further tubbing was required. To achieve this, a scaffolding rig or platform, suspended by two ropes and six chains, was lowered into the shaft by means of a capstan engine. Working on this platform the miners were just 3ft above the water of the flooded shaft, which was 18 yards deep. Passing through a hole in the centre of the platform was a hoppit or suction water barrel used to bring water to the surface whilst work on the tubbing was in progress.

On the night of 7 February 1913, eighteen men were working on the scaffolding. At 7.30 p.m. disaster struck when a suction barrel full of water came crashing down the shaft. The barrel, weighing over 5 tons, smashed through the platform sending debris and thirteen men plummeting into the freezing water at the bottom of the shaft. Many of the men may have been killed instantly by the impact, whilst others who were stunned, drowned before regaining their senses. Five men, all of whom were severely injured, managed to cling to the remnants of the platform. Their ordeal lasted for about an hour before they were rescued. Sadly one of the survivors died five days later as the result of his injuries, bringing the death toll up to fourteen.

What had caused this tragic event? The shift had been working for a full 5 hours before the accident and the manager and master sinker had visited the work an hour before. An inquiry into the accident and deaths revealed that it was a bizarre chain of events in the winding engine house on the surface which had led to the accident.

The winding gear of a colliery was operated by an engineman, from a chair set in front of control leavers. This was skilled work requiring a degree of concentration. Around a week before the accident, a violent gale had loosened the slates of the winding house roof. This had allowed the rain water to seep in under the tiles and run down onto the horizontal beams supporting the roof. Rain was also coming in through the ventilation in the centre of the roof. This produced a constant drip of water directly onto the head of the engineman seated at the controls.

Annoyed by this constant distraction, the engineman at the time, John

Hollingsworth, had taken it upon himself to erect a temporary shelter over the chair. The canopy was constructed by nailing a piece of wood either side of the chair which projected forward above the head of the occupant. Over the two laths was placed a piece of brattice cloth. The roof was later repaired and the cloth was removed.

On the day of the accident another violent storm had caused the roof once again to leak and produce a constant drip of water onto the head of the engine man, Sydney Brown. Brown placed a heavy horse rug (9lbs) over the laths, but this quickly began to sag under its own weight and that of the pooling water. In an attempt to remedy this, Brown laid a heavy plank of wood across the laths under the blanket.

Shortly before the accident, Brown had complained of a problem with the electric lighting in the winding house. Whilst winding the water barrel, he was engaged in a conversation with one of the banksmen (supervisor) about this matter. As the barrel began to approach the top of the shaft and Brown was about to begin breaking, disaster struck. Under the weight of the blanket and accumulated water, the nails holding the laths loosened causing them to tip forward. The rug dropped down over Brown's head and the plank under it slid out and dropped down between the leavers controlling steam brake and throttle. Brown managed to extricate himself from the blanket and, together with the banksman, managed to free the piece of wood from between the leaves. Although Brown shut off the steam and applied the brake, thus preventing an overwind, such was the momentum of the barrel that it continued upwards under its own volition. The barrel struck the beams carrying the bell of the detaching hook and it fell back with such force that the spring hook was pulled open. The barrel now fell back down the shaft, striking one of the cross beams of the headgear nearest the winding engine house and was deflected to the other side where it struck the door of the top landing. It then rebounded back across the shaft, striking the opposite door of the bottom landing. From here it fell 156 yards to the scaffolding below.

The Rufford Colliery began production later in October 1913, after the top hard coal seam had been reach at a depth of 554 yards. The nearby village of Rainworth expanded rapidly when the Company built new housing to accommodate 400 miners and their families. The colliery continued in production for eighty years, finally closing in 1993. The disaster of 1913 was the largest single loss of life in the colliery's history.

❧ NOTTINGHAM'S CAVES ❧

'If a man is poor he had only to go to Nottingham with a matlock, a shovel,
a crow, an iron, a chisel or a mallet, and with such instruments he may play
mole and work himself a hole or burrow for his family'.

Anon., 1870

As anyone who lives in or has ever visited the city knows, Nottingham is built over
a large number of artificial caves. In fact, over 500 have been recorded. Is it a wonder
then that the first ever reference to the city calls it 'Tigguacobauc' – cavy house?

Around the year 868, the Welsh monk Asser, later Bishop of Sherborne,
chronicler to King Alfred, was travelling to Lincoln. He records in his diary:
'This day passed Tigguacobauc.' This word, in his native tongue, is now generally
translated as 'cavy house' and is thought to refer to Nottingham. In those times
a journey to Lincoln would have been along the remains of the old Roman
road, the Fosse Way. The closest this road comes to the city is at Cotgrave, over
12 miles to the south-east. It is doubtful that Asser would have seen even the
largest of caves from that distance with the naked eye. It is more likely that he
simply saw smoke rising from a large settlement across the River Trent and asked
a native guide its name. The resulting Tigguacobauc would therefore be Asser's
own interpretation of what he had been told. All we can say is that there were
caves and people living and working in them at this time.

The Nottingham caves are to be found in groups or clusters in various locations
throughout the city. Not all of them were excavated in Asser's time or were used
as dwellings. For countless generations, local people have taken advantage of the
fact that the native bedrock beneath the city is easily worked soft red sandstone.
It is likely that the first caves for dwellings were excavated in the face of the many
exposed sandstone cliffs like those at Sneinton Hermitage and the Park Estate.
Perhaps the best known and most recognisable of this kind of cave are those of
Castle Rock. The massive rock outcrop on which the castle stands is riddled with
caves, so much so that viewed from a distance it looks like a giant Swiss cheese.

Evidence of the earliest caves to be excavated in Nottingham has probably been
destroyed by constant modification and usage. However, some rock dwellings

or cave houses dating back to around 1250 have been positively identified by finds of domestic pottery and other artefacts. Caves specifically for the use of dwellings continued to be excavated throughout the medieval period and on into the nineteenth century. Records from the 1600s – where they are referred to as 'pauper holes' suggest that these were, in the main, homes for the poor. The use of 'cave houses' – began to decline in 1845, when the 'St Mary's Enclosure Act' banned the renting of cellars and caves as homes for the poor. The simple word 'cave'

The Miller's Cave, Castle Rock. An example of the many multi-storey caves below the castle. (Courtesy of Joe Earp)

is somewhat inadequate to describe the vast network of tunnels and chambers beneath the streets of Nottingham. The sandstone rock acts as a good aquifer and many of the caves have wells supplying water for both domestic and industrial use. Because caves keep a constant temperature, many have been created as cellars and storage facilities.

As Nottingham began to grow and prosper, new caves were excavated to accommodate industry. Beneath the Broadmarsh Shopping Centre is an entire tannery which was in use from 1500 to 1640. To date, twenty–eight malt kiln caves have been recorded. Other caves have been used for the production of pottery, alabaster carving and the brewing industry. In the seventeenth and eighteenth centuries, the demand for sand as a cleaning product increased substantially and Nottingham met that demand. Many thousands of tons of sand were excavated from under the city from new sand mines, resulting in the vast network of caves like those under Peel Street.

The majority of Nottingham's caves lie hidden from public view. However, if you would like to experience the caves for yourself, some, like those at Lenton, are open by request to groups of visitors or on Heritage Days. Highly recommended is a visit to the City of Caves, located in the Broadmarsh Shopping Centre. If you can't make a trip to Nottingham, you are now able to take a stunning virtual tour of the caves on line, courtesy of 3D laser scans. The scans are part of Trent and Peak Archaeology's comprehensive cave survey which is currently being conducted by Dr David Strange Walker and his team.

My maternal grandfather, before the Second World War, lived in a house on Raleigh Street, Radford, in the western suburbs of the city. A short flight of stairs in the cellar of the house led to a cave tunnel which in turn led into a network of further tunnels. Exploring these tunnels, my grandfather found that they emerged in both the Rock Cemetery caves and cellars under the houses of the Park Estate. For obvious reasons my grandfather kept the door to the cave tunnel locked and what lay beyond a close family secret.

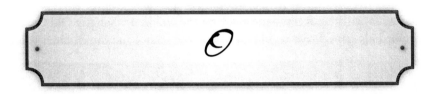

⚜ OLD GENERAL (THE), NOTTINGHAM'S ⚜
MOST CELEBRATED ECCENTRIC

One of the most popular public houses in Nottingham was the Old General, situated on the corner of Bobbers Mill Road and Radford Road in Hyson Green, a suburb of the city. Outside, above the ornate front door, encased in a colonnaded glass-windowed cubical, is a life-size statue of a rather humpbacked man in eighteenth-century dress. Each year, around Christmas, successive landlords decorated the cubical and the statue was donned with a Santa Claus outfit. The statue is that of the Old General from which the house takes its name.

The Old General, whose real name was Benjamin Mayo, was no military man. He was, in fact, Nottingham's most famous and well-loved eccentrics. Mayo was born around 1779 in Nottingham and lived most of his life with his mother. Nearly 100 years later in 1877, the well-respected Nottingham historian Potter Briscoe described Mayo's appearance in great detail

> He was very round shouldered and his stature was no more than four feet high. His eyes were dark grey and his forward was very prominent. He wore his shirt unbuttoned revealing his copper coloured chest. It was said that his legs were badly deformed so that his progress, which was generally a jog-trot, was very peculiar.

Most people regarded Mayo as 'simple minded' and others referred to him as a 'half-wit'. Although he was clearly born with a degree of physical disability, it is unlikely that he had what we would now term learning difficulties. In fact, he was very clever and many amusing tales are told of how he earned a living through his wits.

Within the confines of Nottingham, Mayo regarded his authority as second only to that of the mayor. His title of 'General' comes from his activities on Mickleton Monday – the first Thursday in September – when the Mickleton jury were accustomed to beat the bounds of the town. The jury would proceed through the streets of the town to take note of any obstruction or irregularities. It was then that he was at the height of his glory and Mayo became a 'General'.

Marshalling the school children of the town into military order he would parade them after the jury on its perambulations, prepared to remove any offending obstacle immediately. It was a great day for the children when the Old General assembled his army. Mayo would turn up at the school and the children would

Portrait of Benjamin Mayo, the 'Old General'. (Courtesy of the Paul Nix Collection)

demand a holiday. Most were granted their wish and the 'troops' moved on to the next school. Whenever a schoolmaster refused to allow their pupils to join the growing force, the army would besiege the school and mud and stones would be plentiful thrown. However, the Old General was always open to bribes and 'two pence' would usually buy him off. The proceedings terminated with the Old General and his army demanding entrance to Nottingham Castle. This was always refused but it became customary for sweetmeats to be thrown over the gateway for the children to scramble for.

The Old General was always keen to keep his army in good order and he was often seen drilling his troops in the Market Place. On one occasion, a party of army officers from the barracks on the top of the Park came up to watch his parade. One of the Old General's recruits was particularly slow witted and was constantly making mistakes in his drill. Laughingly, an officer said to the Old General, 'What will you do with him? He is too stupid for a soldier.' The Old General said nothing to the officer but called the boy out of ranks and, standing him in an appropriate place, said loudly, 'There lad you'll never make a soldier, you are too stupid, so I'll make an officer of you.'

Mayo often sold 'broadsheets' in the town and on one occasion he went running through the streets calling out, 'Speech by the Prince of Wales, full account of what his Royal Highness said yesterday!' One customer purchased a copy of Mayo's broadsheet and found he had been presented with a blank sheet of paper. Protesting against the imposition he received the reply, 'Quite correct Sir, 'is Royal 'ighness never said now't.'

The Old General's comic antics meant that he was well loved by all classes of Nottingham's citizens and he was never short of attention. When his mother died, Mayo was admitted to St Peter's Poorhouse in Hound's Gate, Nottingham. After St Peter's was closed, its master, Mr Hudson, took him into his own home rather than let him go to the newly built Union Workhouse. After a number of years, Hudson moved away from Nottingham and Mayo was forced to go to St Mary's Workhouse. Mayo did not feel happy here and his health began to deteriorate. As the consequences of a fall, Benjamin Mayo died In January 1843. He was buried with reasonable dignity in St Peter's churchyard, Broad Marsh burialground.

A few years after he died, many of the boys who could remember Mayo from their childhood decided to pay for a plaque to remember him. This they had set up on a wall by a quiet corner of Nottingham's General Cemetery. My son Joseph (Joe), also an historian, visited the General Cemetery early in 2013. To his horror he found that the plaque was in quite a bad state of repair. It had become detached from the wall and was on the floor covered in leaves and general rubbish. Through Joe's appeal to Nottingham Civic Society the plaque was returned to its rightful place on the wall where it remains as it was intended, a tribute to one of Nottingham's best-loved characters.

❧ OLD STONES OF NOTTINGHAMSHIRE (THE) ❧

Of all Nottinghamshire's natural curiosities the most impressive are its three Old Stones – a title I bestowed upon them as a collective name. They are in fact natural geological features, although there is still some dispute about one of them. Individually, like three wise old men, they are all very different and each has lived a very different life. One thing they have in common is that they have acted like magnets to the generations of curious humans who have shared and now share the landscape in which they stand.

Let me introduce the Old Stones. In order of size they are: the Himlack, the Crumlech Stone and the Cromlech Stone, or Hemlock Stone as it is now called, which stands on the eastern slope of Stapleford Hill, Bramcote. The Alter, Blidworth Rock, the Druid's Stone and simply the Druid Stone are all names given to the Old Stone which stands in the parish of Blidworth. Bob's Rock is the name given to the stone in Stapleford parish.

The Hemlock Stone

> 'What eyes innumerable, O ancient stone,
> have gazed and gazed thy antique form upon?'
>
> *Henry Septimus Sutton*

So wrote H.S. Sutton concerning an enigmatic sandstone outcrop at Bramcote near Nottingham, popularly called the Hemlock Stone. In Sutton's poem, he speaks proudly of the countless generations who have stood by its brooding bulk 'from woad-dyed savage' he says, 'to the gentleman in his carriage passing by.' Legend has it that the Hemlock Stone was hurled by the Devil from Castleton in Derbyshire at a pious monk in Lenton Priory some 4 miles west of the stone.

Geologically speaking, the Hemlock Stone is a pillar consisting of many layers of Sherwood sandstone deposited in the Triassic period 250 to 200 million years ago. The top two layers have been permeated by the mineral baryte (barium sulphate), turning it into green sandstone – which is now blackened with age. These have resisted weathering and overhang the underlying strata, giving the whole a mushroom-like shape, 30ft high and 70ft in circumference at its base.

There are three schools of thought concerning how the stone came into being. The first is that it is the by-product of quarrying. This idea was spawned by the earliest written reference to the stone. The antiquarian William Stukeley passed by or was informed about the stone during his visit to Nottingham in 1722. He passed the comment that 'it is probably the remains of a quarry dug from around it'. Thorsby, in his work of 1790, perpetuates this idea by repeating Stukeley's words. The second theory continues the quarrying idea, suggesting that it was deliberately excavated by some ancient civilization as a symbol of worship or celebration. The third and more plausible theory is that the stone is the product of nature, the result of natural erosion.

The origins of the name(s) of this Old Stone are much disputed. The simplest explanation for the name Hemlock Stone is given in the oral tradition that local witches, who met at the stone, are said to have gathered the poisonous plant hemlock, which once grew around the site, for use in their rites.

The name Hemlock may derive from a combination of two Anglo-Saxon words, *hemm*, meaning border, and *loca*, an enclosure. Hemlock Stone would thus translate as 'the stone in the border field'. A ninth-century Danish or Viking origin is suggested, if we believe the name Hemlock to be a corruption of the old Danish word *hemmelig*, meaning a cover or overhanging.

In some accounts, the name is said to be a corruption of Crumlech or Cromlech Stone, a name which is derived from seventeenth-century Welsh and translates as 'a bent flat stone'. This suggests an early Celtic or Iron Age origin for the name, which has been anglicised or corrupted to Hemlock.

The Hemlock Stone. The scaffolding goes up in preparation for 3D laser scanning the stone as part of the Three Stones Project. (Courtesy of Joe Earp)

Another Saxon origin is suggested for the stone's alternative name, the Himlack Stone. This is similar to the German *Himmel-axt-stein* – Heaven, hatched, stone – used to describe similar geological features like the Devil's Table in Germany.

From the time of Stukeley's first reference to the present day, almost every antiquarian historian and folklorist has written about the Hemlock Stone. Many early writers have speculated that the stone represented Druidical remains – in modern terms it was a part of a much wider prehistoric ritual landscape.

Dr Spencer Timothy Hall (1812–1885), aka The Sherwood Forester, provides us with reasons for believing that the Hemlock Stone was once venerated by our pagan forefathers. The good doctor believed the stone to be of natural origin but to be man-enhanced, the result of deliberate quarrying. He goes on to say that when he was a young boy the old folk could remember a time when a fire was lit upon the top of the stone annually on Beltane Day (1 May).

The Hemlock Stone has drawn visitors to Stapleford Hill for centuries. One of these was the Nottinghamshire author D.H. Lawrence, who as a teenager in 1903 visited the stone with his friends. Lawrence went on to include a reference to the stone in *Sons and Lovers*:

> They came to the Hemlock Stone at dinner-time. Its field was crowded with folk from Nottingham and Ilkeston. They had expected a venerable and dignified monument. They found a little, gnarled, twisted stump of rock, something like a decayed mushroom, standing out pathetically on the side of a field.

Although Lawrence's description of the stone is not a favourable one, the crowd of visitors gives an idea of its popularity.

Now a part of Bramcote Park – administered by Broxtowe Borough Council – the stone is still a popular visitors' attraction. On 3 June 2002 a large bonfire was lit on the top of the Hemlock Stone. This served as part of the worldwide chain of 2,006 beacons lit in celebration of the Golden Jubilee of Queen Elizabeth II. Since that day, the crowds gather around the same time for each for an annual event called the Hemlock Happening.

The Druid Stone

'A thousand malisons on his devoted head who may here after diminish or remove an particle of the relic known as the Druid's Stone.'

Reverend H.R. Whitworth

A fraction over 9 miles north of the Hemlock Stone lies the county's second largest Old Stone. The stone is now commonly called the Druid Stone, but at the time of the first written reference, appears to have simply been referred to as the Rock (Blidworth Rock). The antiquarian Major Hayman Rooke – who gave his name to Sherwood's famous Major Oak – visited Blidworth in 1786 and through Thorsby's work published in 1790, is the first to furnish us with a description and opinion of the stone; 'Near Blidworth, on Sherwood Forest, is a singular Rock'. The accompanying illustration is labelled 'Blidworth Rock'. Thorsby says, 'The only account Mr Rooke could get of it was, that it has been there since time immemorial.' Thorsby goes on to say that Rooke is certain that the cave or hollow cut into the western face of the stone is the product of human hands, but cannot decide as to whether the stone itself is of art (man-made) or not. However, Thorsby goes on to say, 'Mr R. cannot help thinking, that, this very singular rock would not pass unnoticed by the superstitious Britons.'

By the time of the next reference to the stone in 1873, Blidworth Rock had become firmly associated with the Druids and the Revd Richard H. Whitworth, vicar of Blidworth from 1865 to 1908, calls it the 'Druid's Stone or Alter'. He goes on to describe it as being 'like a tombstone of past ages and generations, one of the most remarkable and interesting of all the associations with Sherwood'. Later, he calls down a curse on anyone who would damage or interfere with the stone. So ingrained was the Druid connection, the first edition of the O.S. map – published in 1836 – marks the site simply as 'Druidical Remains'. Cornelius Brown in his *History of Nottinghamshire*, whilst mentioning the Hemlock Stone by name, also simply refers to the Druid Stone as 'Druidical Remains'.

There are no references referring to the stone as the Druid Stone until the mid- to late 1970s, when the author and P. Hannah begin referring to it as such in various *Earth Mysteries* journals. The name has stuck and is now commonly used for the stone.

The geology of the stone is different from that of the Hemlock Stone. It is an exposed mass, a pillar, of a sedimentary rock type known as conglomerate or pudding stone, measuring 14ft high and 48ft in diameter at its base. Conglomerate, as the name implies, is a rock formed from large clasts (pebbles) cemented together in a finer matrix – in this case sand – the whole resembling a natural concrete. The stone rises from a raised platform of bedrock of similar material. It is believed by geologists that it was created toward the end of the last Ice Age, around 10,000 years ago, by erosion of the surrounding softer material.

It is certain that the hole or cave cut into the western face of the stone is artificial. On entering, the hole is designed to force a restricted view wall to the north-east, through the aperture in the opposite. Whitworth says that this was designed to give a view of the sunrise over a nearby hill on 21 June, Midsummer's Day. However, the alignment is too far north and a field survey by Hannah and professional surveyor Barry Christian proved it to be sunrise on 1 May, Beltane, one of the cross-quarter days of the solar year.

Just north of the stone is a large earth-fast boulder of the same material. This boulder has a notch or channel cut the full length across it upper surface. When viewed from along this notch, the north face of the Druid Stone, combined with the notch, produces an almost complete oval. Another smaller boulder, which I have nicknamed the 'Dragon Stone', sits on the brow of the hill around 100 yards to the north east and marks the opposite point of the sunrise alignment.

Oral tradition tells us that children were passed through the aperture in the stone in an attempted cure for rickets. This practice is said to have given the name to the nearby Rickets Lane.

Whitworth presents us with something of a mystery when in a description of the Druid Stone given to the Association of Archaeological Society's in 1874, he says that the stone was 'once surrounded by attendant masses of similar rock unknown in the district'. By the use of the word 'unknown', is Whitworth implying that these stones were brought in to the district deliberately to enhance the site?

Unfortunately, the Druid Stone is on private land but a good view of the stone may be obtained from the nearby public footpath. However, this may one day become restricted as the owner has recently planted a screen of trees.

Bob's Rock

Until recently, the smallest of the three Old Stones has been largely ignored and the earliest written reference is that of historian Robert Mellors in 1906. No accurate measurements of the stone have ever been taken and it has never made an appearance on any O.S. map.

Bob's Rock is a weathered pudding-shaped pillar, which is the top portion of a broad flat platform of rock created by sand, pebbles and mud washed into a crack or fissure in the older Sherwood sandstone bedrock. Erosion since the end of the last Ice Age has worn away the bedrock and exposed the deposits. Further weathering of the exposed mass has created the shape we see today. It is located on the north-facing brow of a high hill above the small town of Stapleford.

Until the nineteenth century, when the area was heavily sand quarried, it was surrounded by open pasture land. A cave under the southern side – which may have been excavated in prehistory – had an attached lean-to over its mouth and was used as a cattle shed, the remains of which are believed to be stalls or mangers which can still be seen cut into the outside face.

The area is now covered in modern trees, making the stone all but invisible. A fraction under 1 mile to the north-east is the Hemlock Stone, which in the winter, when the surrounding trees are bare of leaves, is clearly seen against a green swath of grass.

The site commands extensive views to the north-west across the Errwash Valley as far as the Derbyshire hills – including Crich Stand. To the west the tall steeple of St Helen's church rises above the site of the ancient ford which gave the town its name. In the churchyard stands one of Stapleford's and the county's treasures, an eighth- or ninth-century Saxon cross. The cross, which once stood in the middle of the road leading to the Errwash, is believed to be the original staple or post, which indicated the fording place. Before the cross was moved to the churchyard, the tall village maypole stood within 4 or 5ft of its base.

Like the stone at Blidworth, Bob's Rock may have been simply referred to as 'The Rock'. The word rock is similar in every language from Celtic, Latin, Anglo-Saxon and Norman-French; *roch*, *rocca*, *rocc* and *roque*. As a prominent landscape feature, Bob's Rock is likely to have been used as a boundary marker. The addition of a personal name to a boundary marker would distinguish it immediately and identify the land owner.

In 1086, twenty years after the Norman Conquest, Stapleford was held for William Peverel by the Norman knight, Robert de Heriz. It is not unreasonable to believe that a stone marking the boundary of de Heriz jurisdiction should assume the title of Robert's Rock. As Bob is a very old derivative of Robert, in the vernacular this would become Bob's Rock.

The area around the main crossroads in the town has for centuries been known as The Roach. This is said to be an Anglicised version of the French *le roche*.

The cave beneath Bob's Rock. Overgrown and neglected, the site was visited by the author in 2013 as part of the Three Stones Project. (Courtesy of Joe Earp)

There is a popular legend that the name comes from the fact that during the Napoleonic Wars, French prisoners of war were set the task of breaking rocks or stones on this site. However, I can find no evidence of French prisoners being held in this district.

Perhaps Bob's Rock's greatest claim to fame is the fact that it was used by the Methodist preacher John Wesley as an outdoor pulpit to preach his message to the people of Stapleford in 1774. Soon after a Methodist chapel was erected at the foot of the hill upon which the stone stands. In honour of the Wesley visit, the site became a popular picnic spot for the Methodist Sunday school.

OLIVER (THE REVEREND GEORGE) AND NOTTINGHAM'S DRUID TEMPLE

This is the story of one man's efforts to preserve what he thought to be an important part of Nottingham's history and something he considered a National Treasure. It is also the story of the clash of two men's ambitions – the Reverend George Oliver and Edwin Patchitt.

The Reverend George Oliver is described as 'one of the most distinguished and learned of English Freemasons'. Oliver was born in the Nottinghamshire village of Papplewick in 1782. He was the eldest son of Samuel Oliver, rector of Lambley, and his wife Elizabeth. Like his father, the young George Oliver was destined for the Church. After receiving what is described as a liberal education he became a deacon in 1813 and was ordained in 1815, taking the post of chaplain to the Bishop of Lincoln.

Oliver's approach to his calling was always a scholarly one. In 1836, at the age of 54, he became a Doctor of Divinity. But Oliver's passions were not only for the Church. From his father he inherited a love of Freemasonry and went on to become one of the foremost Masonic writers. His list of publications are too numerous and involved to cover here. It is important to mention that Oliver's Masonic interest lay in Masonic history and a subject known as Mystic Masonry.

Oliver's passion also lay in ancient history and he must also be considered as an historian and antiquarian. As such, in 1850 he was keeping an eagle eye on work that was taking place on a hill to the north of the city, close to the Mansfield Road – the building of Church Cemetery.

By 1850, the population of the city had grown and along with the need for new housing came the need for other services, one of which was the provision of new burial grounds. Plans were drawn up for a new cemetery to be built on some of the land set aside in 1845. The new burialground was to be called Church Cemetery, and plans included catacombs cut into the natural rock and a large new church which would have rivalled anything in the city.

The land chosen for the new enterprise, described as 'a bare and barren hill', was part of a sandy ridge running roughly east-west. Here, the ancient north-south road out of the city – now the A60, Mansfield Road – traverses the ridge before entering the old Sherwood Forest. Known as Gallows Hill on old maps, the summit was the place of public executions until 1827. The original site of the gallows – which were moved to the steps of the Shire Hall – was just in front of the cemetery gates.

The cemetery now covers more than half of the northern slope of the ridge and overlooks the Forest Recreation Ground, which was developed around the same time from the land covered by the old Nottingham Racecourse.

In order to oversee the building work and facilitate its future operation, the Cemetery Company was formed, which was composed of local businessmen. The clerk to the company – solicitor and future Mayor of Nottingham – Edwin Patchitt, owned a vast track of land known as Patchitt's Park on the opposite side of the road. Whilst the cemetery was under construction, he began to develop this land, building large villas and fashionable houses for the wealthy middle class.

Money for the project began to run out and the over-ambitious plans were cut back. The church was never built and the burialground quickly became known as Rock Cemetery, from the bare sandstone rock into which part of it was cut. The cemetery was still incomplete when it was opened in 1856.

The site was not completely the bare and naked hill described. At the foot of the hill was at least one large cavern known as Robin Hood's Cave or Stable. Tradition has it that this was used by Robin and his outlaw band to hide in and stable their horses. It was from this base that Robin is said to have rescued Will Stutly from the nearby gallows.

The area had also been used for rope making and there were a few rough buildings on the hillside and further small caves, one of which was being used to keep chickens in. On the eastern ridge running west from the road was a line of old post mills (windmills).

As excavation work began around a shallow depression or valley cut into the hill, a number of curious features began to be uncovered from under the layers of accumulated sand. Watching events was the Revd George Oliver. As more and more oddities began to emerge, Oliver thought he saw evidence of a recognisable structure, something he was to later call a 'Druid Temple'.

As a Victorian antiquarian, Oliver's understanding was limited to the knowledge of the age. At this time, the study of pre-history was still in its infancy. Victorian's like Oliver took much of their information on pre-history from three main sources: the Bible, Roman writers like Julius Caesar and Tacitus, and antiquarians of the previous generation like William Stukeley (1687–1765). As a Mystic Freemason, Oliver's view of pre-history was particularly coloured by the work of Stukeley, a fellow Mason.

In Oliver's day, antiquarians had not developed the modern archaeological practice of dividing the past into separate periods – Neolithic, Bronze Age, Iron Age etc. Victorian antiquarians and their predecessors considered that before the Romans arrived in Britain there had been but a single culture, which they referred to as the 'Ancient British'. In reality, pre-Conquest Britain (the Iron Age), along with most of Continental Europe, was populated by a highly sophisticated people known as the Celts. Caesar, in his work *The Gallic Wars*, states that the priesthood of the Celts were the Druids, who were 'concerned with divine worship, due performance of sacrifices, public and private, and the interpretation of ritual questions.' With this in mind, Oliver and his fellow antiquarians considered that any religious or ritual site – like a stone circle or burial mound – in their 'Ancient Britain' must have been built by the Druids.

Much of Oliver's work involves what Freemasons call the Spurious Freemasonry of Antiquity. Freemasons believe that rituals and doctrine are subject to the divine influence of a single God and consider this to be what they call True Freemasonry. In an ancient past, Noah reviled the secrets of Freemasonry to the Pagans who corrupted it to a less pure form. Oliver and his fellow Freemasons believed that the Druids where practitioners of Spurious Freemasonry.

Oliver considered himself well qualified to pass an opinion on what was being revealed at the cemetery building site. Something he believed to be the remains of 'a dilapidated structure of an age approximating on 3,000 years.' This emerging structure he saw as an ancient sacred or ritual site and therefore a Druid Temple. If considered today by a modern scholar it would have been classified as being Neolithic or Bronze Age.

Between 1858 and 1859, Oliver addressed his concerns over the remains on the cemetery site in a series of seven 'open letters' to Patchitt, who by this time had become Lord Mayor of Nottingham, an office in which he served two conservative terms. These letters were later published in a book entitled *Shadows Departed: A Few Conjectures on the British Antiquities in Nottingham and Vicinity*.

This was by no means the first time Oliver had written on such a subject. In 1846 he published a letter addressed to Baronet Sir Edward Bromhead, prominent landowner and mathematician, under the title of *The Existing Remain of the Ancient Britons within a small district lying between Lincoln and Sleaford*.

Within a year of the publication of Oliver's *Shadows Departed*, a book entitled *A Guide to the Druid Temple* was published anonymously. Whether this was the work of Oliver himself or some enterprising person cashing in on Oliver's supposed discoveries is debatable.

Despite the fact that the land was virtually wasteground, clearing it proved no easy task. Particularly difficult was the area around the shallow depression at the eastern end adjacent to the road. Here was the 'old rope-walk' – a rope-making site – a few tumbled-down buildings, a number of small caves and the large and complex 'Robin Hood's Stable'.

Thousands of tons of sand were slowly removed from the hollow, revealing that it was no minor natural scar in the landscape but a large and complicated manmade feature. It proved to be a massive rectangular enclosure cut horizontally into the hillside – running north-south parallel with the Mansfield Road. The northern terminus is open with views across the forest to 'Sunrise Hill' at Bestwood.

Oliver gives the dimensions of this enclosure as being 140 yards in length, terminating to the south in a semi-circular end 35 yards in diameter. The two long sides are bounded by cliffs which gradually increase to the south to a height of over 40ft. Oliver calls this southern terminus The Head of the Temple. The northern end (short side) was open with views across the forest to Sunrise Hill at Bestwood. The cliff face on the western side was cut through with caves, one of which is Robin Hood's Stable.

Running down the centre of the enclosure is what Oliver describes as a 'serpentine path'. This path had been cut through the bedrock over 3ft deep and 6ft wide. It was lined on either side by thirty pits which were found to be generally rectangular in shape and varied in depth from 6in to 1ft. Oliver believed these to be holy water tanks where the Druids performed their ritual ablutions. At the southern end the path divided into two, with one branch arcing west towards the mouth of Robin Hood's Stable, and the other east to stone arches which appeared to have been the broken remains of further caves. Oliver saw this path as the Druidical image of a two-headed winged serpent. He goes on to relate this to William Stukeley's interpretation of the Avenue at Avebury.

Within the semi-circular area at the northern end – Oliver's Head of the Temple – were a number of curious features, again all hewn out of the solid rock. At the centre of the semi-circle was a large stone table with a rectangular shallow pit at its foot. To Oliver this was the High Altar of the Temple and the place of human sacrifice, with the pit at the base collecting the blood of the victim.

A few feet behind the altar was a large pillar with a semi-circular notch cut into the top giving the whole a forked appearance. Oliver considered this the truncated remains of what he calls the 'Tolman' or 'Idol'. He believed that the pillar was originally considerably higher and that the notch the bottom half of the hole cut through it.

Perhaps the most curious find in this area was what Oliver describes as the 'Rocking Stone'. Natural rocking stones are geological features, where erosion has caused a large boulder to be perfectly balanced on the surface of the ground. These boulders can be rocked by the slightest touch, but not toppled. Antiquarians and folklore have connected many examples of rocking stones with the Druids. Oliver believed that the Rocking Stone had been deliberately engineered by the builders of the temple. He states that the workmen experienced great amusement in rocking the stone, but found that they needed considerable effort to eventually overturn it and subsequently break it up.

Oliver declares that the entrance to the temple was through a now missing cave at the northern end of the enclosed space. On the eastern side of this end, there can still be seen the broken remains of a cave or tunnel, which Oliver says once extended under the Mansfield Road. Here it emerged as 'a spacious cavern capable of holding over two hundred people'. The land on this side of the road was owned by Edwin Patchitt and as part of his ambitious plans for the city he developed an estate of large of both villas known as Patchitt's Park. When work on the estate began, 160 skeletons of undetermined age were discovered close to the mouth of this cave. Oliver declares these to be the dead of an ancient battle.

The north-eastern side of the enclosure was also found to contain the broken remain of a small cave which Oliver refers to as the 'Archdruids Private Cell'. Here he suggests that the Archdruid conducted ceremonies within the temple, whilst sat enthroned on the mound above the cell. Close to the cell is a curious feature, which today is still visible from the road. It consists of three pillars of rock around 15ft high, which merge together at the top forming an enclosed triangular space. Oliver believed this to be the remains of a dolman (the remains of Neolithic burial mounds, which consist of three upright stone pillars roofed over by a flat capping stone). All that can be said here is that this feature certainly now resembles a dolman which has been cut from bedrock rather than made of individual stone. Whether it was originally engineered as such, as Oliver suggests, is of course debatable.

Although Oliver included no archaeological evidence from the site to support his Druid temple hypothesis, he mentions the discovery of a Bronze Age 'hoard' found by workmen on Great Freeman Street, close to its junction with St Ann's Well Road. The find site Oliver says was 'on eminence halfway along the line between the Temple and Sneinton Hermitage'.

Along with a description of his Druid Temple, Oliver makes great effort to place it into the surrounding landscape. He declared that the site is at the apex of an isosceles triangle with sides of over a mile and a quarter long. The base of this triangle is formed by the line between the caves of the Papish Holes to the west and Sneinton Hermitage to the east. These three cave systems do in fact form a triangle although a modern satellite map shows that it is not a perfect isosceles.

It is unfortunate that Oliver was unable to support his hypothesis with datable artefacts. However, when describing the triangle of caves he refers to a large hoard of Bronze Age axe heads, spear tips, swords and daggers found by workmen in Great Freeman Street, close to its junction with St Ann's Well Road. The site of this discovery is stated as being on an 'eminence halfway along the line between the Temple and Sneinton Hermitage'. Oliver notes that amongst this hoard of 'war-like implements' were bronze tubes, one of which was over 9in long. These, he suggests, were the ends of a staff of office used by a Druid priest.

As work on the new cemetery continued, the temple was very much utilised and adapted. Many of the temple features described by Oliver can still be seen today and the guidebook first published over 100 years ago still serves its purpose.

The southern end of the temple is now enclosed by the high wall of the cemetery boundary, which here divides it from the Forest Recreation Ground. The temple confines are now entered via a Victorian path running down from the main gates of the cemetery, which are roughly on the site of the former gallows. The path descends the hill along the eastern side of the temple parallel to the Mansfield Road. There are good views from the path of the whole structure. At the bottom of the slope the path enters into the temple confines at its south-east corner and joins the serpentine path. In the opposite corner there can be seen the entrance to a long Victorian tunnel created as catacombs. The tunnel is the only entrance to St Anne's Valley, a large semi-circle space enclosed by rock cliffs, originally cut to contain the grave of Nottingham's elite. However, for some reason the valley did not have the appeal that was intended and it now contains paupers' graves.

The serpentine path is today lined on either side by Victorian grave monuments of all shapes and sizes. One of these is that of Edwin Patchitt. Ironically, Patchitt chose to be buried in a spot which Oliver considered to be the temple's 'Holy of Holies', close to the dolman and Archdruid's private cell, both of which can still be seen. Amongst the many grave monuments which today cover the temple floor, Oliver's holy water tanks can still clearly be seen lining the route of the central path as they did when the area was first exposed.

The southern end still contains all of the features Oliver described. The large cave complex of Robin Hood's Stable is deemed unsafe and there is no public access. However, the yawning cave mouths are still an impressive sight.

Was the Revd Dr George Oliver looking through the eyes of faith when he viewed the Church Cemetery site? Others saw his Druid temple as nothing more than the remains of a medieval bleach works and thought the caves to be the product of nothing more than sand mining. I will leave the reader to make their own decision as to whether this is the case.

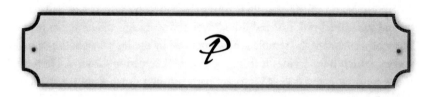

❧ PATIENT NO. 9 ❧

The strangest case in the long history of Nottingham's General Hospital is perhaps that of Katherine (Kitty) Hudson. Kitty was the ninth patient to be admitted to the newly opened hospital on 4 August 1783. Her case caused much excitement in the medical profession and perhaps a little disbelief.

Kitty was born in the Nottingham village of Arnold in 1765, the granddaughter of Mr White, sexton of St Mary's church, Nottingham. At the age of 6, she was sent to live with her grandfather, where to earn her keep she was put to the task of sweeping the pews and aisles of the church. Whilst carrying out her work, every time she found a pin or needle, Kitty would put it into her mouth for safe-keeping. This in itself is not an uncommon practice and perhaps the young Kitty had seen her mother do this whilst carrying out needlework. However, Kitty began to enjoy the sensation of sharp objects in her mouth. This habit was further encouraged by a resident servant girl in her grandfather's employment. For amusement, this young woman would offer Kitty a 'stick of tuffy' in return for a mouthful of pins.

For Kitty, what began as a habit soon became an addiction and, in her own words, 'she could neither eat, drink, nor sleep, without pins or needles in her mouth.' Such was the damage caused by this practice, that by the time her friends and family were aware, she had worn away her double teeth almost to her gums.

Kitty began to suffer a constant numbness in her arms and legs which the doctors could not explain. When she was finally admitted to hospital, Kitty's right arm was inflamed and infected. On examination, the doctors discovered two needles under the skin a little above the wrist. These were quickly extracted using forceps. Further examination revealed more needles higher up the arm, which were also extracted.

With the exception of two or three short breaks when she was sent home, Kitty was to spend nearly two years in hospital until finally discharged as cured. Over this time the records show that she underwent numerous operations and 'great numbers of pins, needles and pieces of carious bone were extracted from her feet, legs, arms and other parts of her body and both breasts were removed with the knife.'

As an in-patient, Kitty's pains continued in various parts of her body and on 11 October the hospital recorded that 'a very large darning needle was this day extracted from her right breast, seemingly buried within a part of that gland; thinks she feels another needle very deep seated under the gland in the middle of the breast; complained of great pain in the breast after the removal of the needle, which in about an hour afterwards became so excessive as to through [*sic*] her into convulsions.'

The convulsions continued intermittently until 1 November, when the records state: 'The needle still appearing to lie very deep within the breast; and about three days ago her jaw became locked; very weak and low; pulse small and weak; made an incision quite through the breast, and extracted a large needle which adhered to the tendinous fascia covering the pectoral muscle; afterwards brought the lips of the wound together with adhesive plaisters.'

Kitty was not just having pins and needles extracted from various parts of her body, but also expelled them in her urine. The records state that on 3 February she 'passed a pin yesterday by urine, which was not coated or particularly corroded [which suggests that other examples may have been] and this day with the same excretion, passed a needle.' Kitty's general condition is described as 'faint and low'.

She again passed a needle in her urine on 4 February. On 11 February she brought up a needle in her vomit and on the 14th had a needle extracted from her breast.

On 24 February, Kitty's right breast again became extremely inflamed, which continued for several days. By 8 March, Kitty was complaining of a deep-seated pain in her breast which prevented her from resting. Without doubt, the doctors suspected the pain to be caused by yet another needle and on 19 March were planning to operate in order to remove it.

During the operation – which took place on the 22nd – the needle, passed into Kitty's thorax and could not be reached. Her breast tissue was found to be so infected that part of it was removed.

The records for 26 June state: 'For several days [she] has complained of great pain in her breast and describes it to be as if several pins were lodged in the mamma and pectoral muscle, and lying between the two ribs.'

On the morning of 30 August Kitty was once again operated on and the whole of her right breast was removed. On examination, a needle was found in the middle of the tissue. In the evening, Kitty suffered a haemorrhage and the dressings were removed and a pin was found in the dressing.

Still complaining of pain, Kitty's dressings were again partially removed on 4 September and a pin was found sticking to them with four more pins lodged in the wound. Two more pins were found stuck to the dressing on the 9th and a further two and a plum-stone – which she had swallowed two days before – on the 11th.

Kitty Hudson's case continued to fascinate and baffle the medical staff at Nottingham's General Hospital throughout the remainder of 1783 and for most of 1884. Many more needles and pins were removed or spontaneously erupted from various parts of her body and her left breast also became badly infected.

Kitty Hudson as a postwoman. (Author's Illustration)

Kitty was finally discharged from hospital as fully 'cured' on 27 December 1884. But her story has a somewhat surprising and relatively happy ending.

By coincidence, a young man by the name of Goddard attended the hospital as an out-patient, with what is described in the records simply as a 'complaint in the head' – through which he lost an eye. This young man was also from Arnold and was a childhood friend of Kitty's. Later, Kitty was to comment that he 'had sweethearted her from a child.' The two quickly renewed their friendship and became romantically attached. Goddard swore that he would marry Kitty even if she lost all her limbs, providing her life was spared.

They were married six months after Kitty's discharge from hospital and lived in Arnold. Here, Kitty bore nineteen children, only one of which – a daughter, who lived until the age of 19 – survived infancy. Kitty became the Nottingham Post (postwoman) and for many years walked twice daily between Arnold and Nottingham. A popular figure, she is described as being 'tall, stout and of masculine appearance'. Carrying her large leather postbag over her shoulder, she wore a small bonnet, a man's spencer (a short tailless jacket) of drab cloth, a coarse woollen petticoat, worsted stockings, and strong shoes.

Kitty's husband died in 1814, and a short time after she went to stay with friends in Derbyshire, where she lived out the remainder of her life.

⁜ QUEEN'S JESTER (THE), WILLIAM WALLETT ⁜ 'ENGLAND'S LAST FOOL'

Many people will be familiar with the idea of the medieval court jester or fool in cap and bells; men like Rehere, court jester to Henry I. However, it might be surprising to know that English monarchs retained the role of court jester long after the medieval period. Perhaps the most famous of these men (and sometimes women) was William 'Will' Sommers, court jester to Henry VIII, and Jeffrey Hudson and Muckle John, court jesters to Charles I. Jesters were entertainers, skilled in the arts of music, juggling and clowning. The days of the court jester came to an end with Oliver Cromwell and the Commonwealth – Charles II did not reinstate the role of court jester/fool. But we should add one more name to this illustrious list of famous fools and Royal Jester, that of William Wallett.

Although William Fredrick Wallett was born in Hull – probably in June or July 1813 – it is Beeston in Nottinghamshire which claims him as its adopted son. William was an internationally famous stage and circus performer. He was the eldest son of John and Margaret Wallett who went on to have a family totalling seven children, five boys and two girls. Both lived into their 80s, long enough to witness and become immensely proud of the success of their eldest son. In fact, on the census of 1871, his mother, Margaret, by then a widow, listed herself as 'Queen Victoria's jester's mother'.

William is described as being athletically built, tall and handsome. He was intelligent and extremely quick-witted. All of these natural attributes he was to use to great effect in taking him to the top of his chosen career in the performing arts. However, even the best has to start at the bottom of the ladder and William began his working life as a scenery painter, odd-job man and 'jobbing-actor' before his talents were recognised.

In 1839 at the age of 26, William married his first wife, Mary Orme, in Lincoln. According to the *Nottingham Review* of 26 April 1839, the marriage was in fact the result of an elopement. Mary's father, a Hull publican, pursued his daughter to the wedding venue and the journal states: 'Shortly after the completion of the ceremony, the happy pair experienced an unwelcome interview with the father of the bride, accompanied by a constable, whose object was to take home, by physical force, the lady, who had left her father's house without his consent. The parties have since become reconciled.'

By this time, William's career had begun to take shape and he had become a circus and stage entertainer with a speciality as a clown. But he was no ordinary clown. William based his act on that of the traditional fool, a satirist who was able to transcend the norms of convention. To this end, he even adopted the costume of the jester, rather than the usual baggy trousers and makeup of the clown. William did not neglect any of his other skills, both circus and theatrical. He continued to appear in stage productions and theatrical reviews and in the circus as an equestrian (bare-back rider) as well as a clown.

William's ambition combined with his talent and flexibility as a performer meant that he became a great success. Travelling throughout the world and in particular the United States, his wit and humour turned him into an international star. However, success came at a great cost to his twenty-two-year marriage.

Mary was left alone for long periods of time whilst William was 'on tour'. When she died at the age of 40 in June 1861, William was performing his equestrian act – probably in America. We do not know if Mary's early death was sudden or the result of a long illness, but the census return of 1861 shows that William was alone at a lodging in Manchester in April of that year. Records show that the couple had at least two children who did not survive infancy.

William Wallett was the master of self-promotion and in July 1844 he pulled off a stroke of genius which made him a household name. At this time, William was performing his clown routine as a part of the famous Van Amburgh Company. On 19 July, the company put on a royal performance at Windsor Castle in front of Queen Victoria and Albert, the Prince Consort. Also attending was the Duke of Wellington and a number of other worthies of the day.

The show was apparently well received and in the following publicity, Wallett declared himself to be the 'Queen's Jester'. The queen must have been amused, because although she did not officially sanction the title, William was not carried off to the Tower in royal disgrace.

Wallett, now the self-proclaimed Royal Jester, is said to have employed only two kinds of promotional posters – a stock of which he kept in the cellar of his house. The first poster, used prior to the engagement, simply read 'Wallett is coming', and the second 'Wallett is here'.

In March 1862, a year after the death of Mary, William Wallett married Sarah Tutin Farmer, the daughter of John Farmer, a Nottingham businessman and entrepreneur. At the time of the wedding, Farmer is recorded as a publican with a house on Market Street. In reality, together with his three sons, one of whom kept the Clarendon Hotel, he controlled a powerful empire which dominated the Nottingham business and social scene. In fact, the Farmer family controlled most aspects of musical entertainment in the town for over 100 years.

John Farmer would have been no stranger to William, who had visited Nottingham many times in the early years of his career, appearing at the music halls and glee clubs that constituted the popular entertainment of the time. The marriage was another extraordinary boost to William's already successful career, but whether it entirely had the approval of Sarah's father is uncertain. This is borne by the fact that the chosen venue was William's home town of Hull. It was popular convention at the time for a bride to marry in her own parish.

Whatever the true circumstances of the wedding, the couple chose to live in Beeston, Nottinghamshire. They moved into Spring Villa, one of a pair of houses which stood on the corner of Queens Road and Station Road. By 1879, William and Sarah had had two children and the family moved to a new house built on adjacent land. This property is now No. 220 Station Road (corner of Grove Street), where a Blue Plaque declares it to be the home of 'William Fredrick Wallett (The Queen's Jester)'.

William Wallett became the toast of the town, entertaining the 'great and the good' at his Beeston home. Ever the performer, William continued to entertain almost to his death in March 1892. Various census returns for the address demonstrates how diverse William's career had become. In the 1871 census he lists himself as simply 'comedian', in 1881 as a 'professor of elocution' and in 1891 an 'actor and lecturer'. Perhaps he should be best remembered as the 'Queen's Jester, England's Last Fool'.

✦ RESURRECTIONISTS ✦

With the development of the lace and textile trade in the 1700s, the population of Nottingham began to increase. This industrial and population growth saw the area around St Mary's church change from a semi-rural setting, with open spaces and large houses of the gentry, to the urban landscape we know today.

This expansion brought with it many problems, not least of which was where to bury the dead. The parish churchyard rapidly began to run out of space and it was decided new burial grounds were needed. Between 1742 and 1813 three new cemeteries were created on land around Barker Gate.

Known officially as Burial Ground No. 1 – Middle Bury – the first of these was consecrated in 1742. Burial Ground No. 2 – Top Bury – was consecrated in 1786, and Burial Ground No. 3 – Bottom Bury – in 1813.

Alongside the Industrial Revolution, Britain experienced advancement in the medical sciences. To fuel this, more doctors were needed and new medical schools sprang up all over the country, particularly in London and Edinburgh. However, this brought about an unusual and macabre trade – that of bodysnatching.

Graveyards were plundered for the bodies of the recently buried by individuals known as resurrectionists or resurrection men. The cadavers were then sold to medical schools for the new medics to hone their anatomical and surgical skills.

By 1827, Barker Gate had become a bustling community of close-packed terrace houses, two or more chapels, three public houses, a school and a number of shops and small businesses. Events which happened in Barker Gate that year were to cause great distress to the residents of Nottingham.

In November 1826, a man called Smith took up lodgings on Maiden Lane, which ran alongside Middle Bury. On 18 January the following year, Smith took a large hamper to Pickfords for delivery to an address in London. The bookkeeper, Mr White, became suspicious and asked to examine the contents. Smith refused, saying that he must first ask his master ,William Giles, who was waiting with a horse and cart at Bullivants Yard on Leenside.

Smith left the office in great haste, hotly pursued by White and one of Pickfords' porters. In the street, White was quickly joined by Alderman Barber and Constable Jeffries. The four men pursued Smith to his meeting with

Giles and before either could mount the cart, apprehended them. However, both Smith and Giles managed to break free, with Smith losing his jacket in the process.

The pair burst through a nearby house into an alley and were never seen again. White and his posse returned to the office and opened the suspicious hamper. Inside they found the body of an old woman, Dorothy Townsend, and a 3-year-old boy, the son of a local woman, Mrs Rose.

(THP)

Resurrectionists at work. (Courtesy of the Paul Nix Collection)

Word quickly spread about the incident and St Mary's graveyards soon became full of people, many of whom were digging amongst the graves anxious to discover if their loved ones were still interred. Constables were called in and the random search ended, but not before it was discovered that thirty bodies had been stolen.

The subsequent enquiry showed that Smith may have been the ringleader and Giles and another man – who had both been lodging at a pub on Barker Gate – his accomplices. Together, the three men had regularly taken packages to Derby and Loughborough for dispatch to London.

The gravedigger William Davies, aka 'Old Friday', was suspected as being an accomplice, but nothing was ever proven. However, Davies narrowly escaped with his life when he was mobbed by crowds in Nottingham and his home village of Arnold. History does not record what became of Old Friday, but Mrs Townsend and Master Rose were once again laid to rest.

❧ RETFORD AND THE BROAD STONE ❧

The market town of Retford, just over 30 miles north of Nottingham, developed at a point where a track, the ancient north–south highway, forded the River Idle. The settlement probably grew up on the western bank of the river but moved to the eastern bank as this side was less prone to flooding. This move prompted the official administrative name for the town, East Retford. The name of the town appears in a number of old documents, including the Domesday Book, with various spellings, e.g. Redforde. Although there is debate as to the origin of the name, it is likely that it simply refers to 'the red ford' and denotes the colour of the water when the red clay of its bed was disturbed when crossing the river.

The settlement remained a small community until 1105 when Henry I established the Borough of East Retford in order to collect tolls from travellers using the ford. In 1246, Henry III granted the growing town its first charter to hold an annual fair. Edward I extended this charter in 1275, granting the right to hold a Saturday market. For administrative purposes, the town is still known officially as East Retford.

The old town was largely destroyed by a fire in 1528. However, rebuilding took place and the town's prosperity was assured in 1766 when the Great North Road was diverted to pass directly through the town along the ancient highway. Further prosper came ten years later with the building of the Chesterfield Canal in 1777 and again in 1849 with the London to York railway.

Over the years, Retford's growth incorporated smaller communities which became suburbs. These included villages like Ordsall, Babworth and Scrooby. The latter two were villages from which originated many of the Pilgrim Fathers, early settlers in the American Plymouth Colony'.

Standing in the Market Square is a relic of Retford's ancient past, the Broad Stone. The stone is actually the base or plinth of a cross. It formally stood on a slight eminence on the west side of the Idle, known as 'Est croc sic' ('the croc (cross) is so'). A variant and perhaps more accurate spelling of the name is 'Est Croc Sick', which has been translated by one authority as 'East Cross Sike' (sike denotes a watercourse or streamlet). The site was later also known as 'Domine Cross' – perhaps from the Latin *domini*. This may have been the original name of the cross rather than the site. The cross was one of four, which are of uncertain origin, but are at least as old as thirteenth century and are believed to have boundary markers. Writing in 1912, Alfred Stapleton says that 'a second is still preserved in the West Retford churchyard, a third was in the churchyard at Ordsall, the fourth is lost'.

Looking more closely at the possible boundary defined by these crosses, we find that in 1286 the boundary between the lordships of Retford and Little Grihgley is described as 'The Beck; a foss or ditch, extending in length (west) from Est Croc Sick to the waters of the Idle'. This might assume that the cross base in West Retford churchyard directly across the river was the western terminus of the boundary. Of this western stone, Piercy's *History of Retford* (1828) states that it formed part of the churchyard wall and was exactly the same form and dimensions as the Broad Stone. He goes on to say that it 'formerly occupied a place on an elevated piece of ground near the road leading to Barnby Moor, in West Retford Field.' His sketch of the church clearly shows the base and shaft of a cross sticking out above the top of the churchyard wall. Another local historian writing in 1892 says of this cross: 'It has recently been taken out of the wall, and placed within the ground, about two or three feet from its former resting place.'

There are a number of references to the third cross in the churchyard at Orsall, about a mile south-west of the Domine Cross, but no descriptions or illustrations. All of the references to the Retford crosses report a fourth cross as now lost, without giving its location.

Of the four Retford boundary crosses, it is the remains of the Domine Cross, the Broad Stone, which has come to symbolise the town's ancient past. The Broad Stone we see today is only a part of the cross. Using all of the available evidence we can say that originally it would have consisted of a large square base stone – with possible tapered sides – and a square hole cut into the middle of its top surface. Into this hole would have been fixed a square pillar around 4ft to 5ft high – the cross shaft. The whole assemblage may have been mounted on a platform of three or four low steps.

For at least three centuries, possibly more, along with its companions, it served its purpose as a boundary marker. The little eminence on which it stood was on the edge of Sherwood Forest and the cross would have been a popular meeting place or assembly point and even a place of Christian worship.

In the sixteenth century, local legend has it that the Domine Cross became a vital lifeline between the town and the rural population. There are several references to the plague making an appearance in Retford. At these difficult times, it is said that the townsfolk continued their trade with the outside world by using the cross (and possible the other three) as an exchange point. Coins previously washed in vinegar – a primitive disinfectant – were placed on the cross in payment for goods and services.

Another local legend says that in 1665 when the plague raged in London, refugees camping in Sherwood Forest again used the cross as a trading place to buy goods from the town. Certainly, we may give this version of the story some credence. There is evidence which shows Londoners fleeing the plague did travel north into Sherwood Forest along the Great North Road.

The townsfolk of Retford must have formed a great attachment to the cross. At some unrecorded date after these terrible times, the base of the cross was removed into the town and erected in the marketplace. From that time on it became known as the Broad Stone. In 1818, it was once again moved to a new position in the centre of the square. Here it appears to have been placed in an inverted position with the square socket hole on its underside. The town directory of 1832 refers to the Broad Stone as still being on this site. However, the directory of 1853 states: 'The Broad Stone has been removed, and a handsome cast-iron pillar, 22 feet high, bearing 5 lamps, has been erected on the site thereof, around which the corn market is held.' It is said that for a long time after, the older inhabitants of the town continued to call the site the Broad Stone.

In illustrations of the time and as we see it today, the whole monument which constitutes the Broad Stone consists of three stones mounted on a purpose-made plinth. Only the top stone is believed to be the original base of the Domine Cross – the actual Broad Stone. Alfred Stapleton suggests that the other two stones are the remains of a previously unrecorded market cross upon which the Broad Stone was mounted when it was first brought to the square from its forest home.

For a number of years, the Broad Stone appears to have disappeared into hiding. However, the stone was not lost and forgotten. In 1868, Retford's old Town Hall was demolished and a new French-inspired edifice was built to replace it. In 1877 the Broad Stone came out of retirement and was placed on a new plinth directly infront of the Town Hall, where it stands to this day. The inscription on the plinth reads: 'The Broad Stone of the Borough of East Retfors. Restored to the Borough of East Retford by J.A. Gylby Esq. AD 1877.'

❧ ROBIN HOOD PLACE NAMES ❧
IN NOTTINGHAMSHIRE

There are twenty-three English counties, from Westmorland and Yorkshire in the north, to Somerset in the south, where Robin Hood appears as part of the name of a feature or object in the landscape. Most have only one or two examples; however, the counties of Nottinghamshire, Derbyshire and Yorkshire all have numbers running into double figures. And why shouldn't they? After all, didn't Robin come from around these parts?

Buildings

Robin Hood Farm

The farm is around 6 miles north of Nottingham on the Ollerton Road. It is so named on C. and J. Greenwood's 1826 map of the County of Nottingham. The building is associated with a nearby linear earthwork of unknown date, which is named on a Tithe Award around 1840 as 'Robin Hood Bank'.

Caves and Holes in the Ground

Robin Hood's 'Cave − Cresswell Crags

Formally known as Robin Hood's Hall, this natural cave has four chambers connected by short passages. It is the largest of the caves at Creswell Crags, a limestone gorge on the border between Derbyshire and Nottinghamshire. As such, it is by far the oldest of all of the sites with a Robin Hood place name prefix. Creswell Crags is a UNESCO World Heritage Site. Evidence of human occupation − including rock art which dates back over 43,000 and 10,000 years − has been found in these caves. When this particular cave gained a title associating it with Nottingham's famous 'outlaw' is uncertain.

Robin Hood's Cave − Annelsey

A cave at the foot of the Robin Hood Hills is said to have once been the entrance to a vast labyrinth of caves and tunnels, one of which led to Annesley Hall. The cave mouth, which has always been difficult to find, was long ago filled up, supposedly to prevent the unwary from becoming lost amongst the many passages which were reputed to contain wells and running streams of water. Legend says that if perused into the cave by the sheriff or his men, Robin could easily escape his enemies by losing them in this underground world.

Robin Hood's Cave − Ollerton

This cave, a mere scrape in the ground compared to others of the same name − is around 2 miles north of Ollerton in the parish of Walesby. It lies directly on the banks of the River Maun, just above the water. Close by is the old London to York road. Local legend states that Robin and his men would hide in this cave ready to ambush unwary travellers passing along the road above.

Robin Hood's 'Grave' − Mansfield

Although referred to as a grave, this site is in fact a cave around 7 miles north of Mansfield in the parish of Holbeck. The name appears in a Tithe Award of around 1840, but does not feature on any other maps of the county.

Robin Hood's Stable – Nottingham

Just north of the city, alongside the Mansfield Road, is Rock Cemetery. The cemetery is built on the southern slopes of the high ground overlooking the Forest Recreation Ground – the site of Nottingham's famous Goose Fair. The cemetery, originally to be called Church Cemetery, takes its modern name from the fact that many of its graves are located in a rectangular enclosure bounded by high sandstone cliffs. On the north-western side of this enclosed space is a large cave, Robin Hood's Stable, which existed long before the idea of the cemetery was even conceived. The cave mouth leads into a vast underground complex of tunnels on two levels. Accepted opinion has it that this labyrinth is the product of seventeenth-century sand-mining. However, legend says that the cave was used by Robin and his Merry Men to hide in and stable their horses. It was from this base that Robin is said to have rescued Will Stutly from the nearby gallows.

Robin Hood's Stables – Papplewick

This rock-cut edifice is in the grounds of a private house in the village of Papplewick, some 8 miles north of Nottingham. Evidence suggests that the cave was indeed used as a stable from around the fifteenth century, although the body of the cave could have been much earlier. Here legend says that Robin kept one of his fastest horses to patrol 'The King's Great Way' (Mansfield Road). Papplewick was once one of Sherwood Forest's main administration centres. The American writer Washington Irving visited the cave whilst staying with his friend Col. Wildman at Newstead Abbey in 1817. His description is perhaps the most evocative ever given: 'It is in the breast of a hill, scooped out of brown freestone, with rude attempt at columns and arches. Within are two niches, which served, it is said, as stalls for the bold outlaw's horses. To this retreat he retired when hotly pursued by the law, for the place was a secret even from his band. The cave is overshadowed by an oak and alder, and is hardly discoverable even at the present day; but when the country was overrun with forest it must have been completely concealed.'

Other Natural Features

Robin Hood's Acre – Nottingham
The name appears in the 1624–25 Records of the Borough of Nottingham.

Robin Hood's Close – Nottingham
A close or small enclosed pasture described as 'Robynhode Close' in the Nottingham Civic Chamberlains Accounts for 1485, 1486 and 1500. This is the earliest reference to a Robin Hood place name in the county.

Old woodcut of Robin Hood. (Author's Collection)

Robin Hood Hills – Annesley

Once a part of Sherwood Forest, the Robin Hood Hills are a range of hills running roughly east–west, around a mile north of Annesley. They are so named on Chapman and Andre's map of 1775, which contains a Robin Hood's Cave and Robin Hood's Chair. The hills are in the district of Hollin Well which takes its name from a holy well on the south-east slopes. The hills are now covered by a golf course and the spring, which still flows, is close to the 8th tee. Legend has it that Robin kept a lookout for the sheriff whilst sitting on his 'chair' on the top of the highest peak in the range. Also known as the Annesley Hills, a path across the top of the hills was one of the favourite haunts of the poet Lord Byron.

Robin Hood's Meadow – Perlthorpe

A book on 'English Field-Names' contains a reference to there being a Robin Hood's Meadow close to Perlthorpe – 2 miles north of Ollerton.

Robin Hood's Hill – Oxton

Also mistakenly called 'Robin Hood's Pot' or 'Pit', the hill is an artificial mound, a Bronze Age tumulus close to Oldox earthwork 1 mile north of Oxton.

Stones

Robin Hood's Chair

Robin Hood's Chair is an artificial rock-cut feature rather than a stone or boulder. Again, it is to Irving that we must turn for our best description:

> Another of these rambling rides in quest of popular antiquities, was to a chain of rocky cliffs, called the Kirkby Crags, which skirt the Robin Hood hills. Here, leaving my horse at the foot of the crags, I scaled their rugged sides, and seated myself in a niche of the rocks, called Robin Hood's chair. It commands a wide prospect over the valley of Newstead, and here the bold outlaw is said to have taken his seat, and kept a look-out upon the roads below, watching for merchants, and bishops, and other wealthy travellers, upon whom to pounce down, like an eagle from his eyrie.

The original 'chair' is believed to have been destroyed by workmen building the Great Central railway line whilst cutting the Kirby to Annesley tunnel around 1849. The feature we see today is the replacement.

Robin Hood's Cross – Pleaseley

A number of seventeenth-century documents refer to a 'Robin Hood's Cross' located in Pleaseley. It is likely that this was the cross erected around 1284 by the then Lord of the Manor, Thomas Bek, after being granted a charter by the king to hold a market and two fairs. The remains of the cross can still be seen on its site close to Pleaseley Mill.

Robin Hood's Stone

The only historical reference to this stone is John Ogilby's map of 1675. A newspaper article from 1912 claims that the stone still existed, but there is no supporting evidence of this fact. The stone's position on the map indicates that it was beside the old Mansfield Road, which formally ran through the grounds of Newstead Abbey. This would place the stone somewhere around the modern gates to the abbey. The stone was likely to have been one of the Great Guide Stones which marked the old Mansfield Road's progress through the wilds of Sherwood Forest.

Robin Hood's Piss-Pot – Oxton

This was a basin-shaped stone and is likely to have been the base of a wayside cross. The stone was some 11 miles north of Nottingham and stood on the eastern side of the A614 Ollerton Road just south-west of the crossroads between Oxton and Blidworth. It marks a point exactly halfway between the two villages and may once have been a part of a parish boundary. The stone is marked on Sanderson's map of 1835 and on the 1836 O.S. map, but not on the 1899 edition.

Robin Hood's Whetstone

Whetstones were and are used for sharpening edged implements, like blades and arrows, and if the name is to be believed this former boundary stone was used for that purpose by Robin Hood. Along with the Abbot's Stone – further north-east and closer to Rufford Abbey – this and several other un-named stones once marked the important boundary between the abbey and the Royal Forest of Clipstone. It appears on a 1630 estate map as a parish boundary marker or 'meer stone'. The stone stands next to the old Mansfield to Tuxford Road (part of the Great North Road), now a forest track. The site is marked by a small stone bearing the letter 'R' on one face.

Trees

Robin Hood's Larder

Also known as the Shambles Tree or Shambles Oak, 'Robin Hood's Larder' was an ancient hollow oak tree in the Birklands area of Sherwood Forest around 3 miles west of Ollerton. The hollow interior contained a number of iron hooks from which Robin is said to have hung venison and other wild meat. However, it is unlikely that the tree was anything more than a sapling in the days of Robin Hood and the hooks were a relic of much later hunting parties. The tree was badly damaged by storms in the 1960s, leading to its demolition.

Wells and Springs

Robin Hood's Well – Beauvale

The well is in High Park Wood around 7 miles north-west of Nottingham. The historian Sloane says it is only '…a bowshot from Beauvale Priory'.

✥ SHEPPHERD, ELIZABETH (BESSIE): ✥
A MURDER ON THE MANSFIELD ROAD

The murder of a young Papplewick girl on the Mansfield Road in 1817 is one
that still resonates with us today. It is perhaps for this reason that over the past few
years it has become one of the best-known tales from the Mansfield Road. It is
also yet another story where the road itself runs like a thread through its narrative
and the lives of all those involved. The murder is well documented and I have a
number of accounts to build up an accurate picture of the events that happened
nearly 100 years ago.

Elizabeth Sheppherd, familiarly known as Bessie, is described in the handbill
produced at the time of the execution of her murderer as 'an interesting girl
about 17 years of age and the daughter of a woman residing at Papplewick'. Other
accounts suggest her to be a pretty girl and an average teenager of her time.

On 7 July 1817, Bessie left her home at about midday to walk to Mansfield,
where she was hoping to find employment in service. She was dressed in her
Sunday best and was wearing a new pair of shoes and carrying a yellow umbrella.
Bessie was successful in her endeavours and witnesses saw her leaving Mansfield
at around 6 o'clock that evening.

Bessie's mother waited patiently for her daughter's return, but as evening
began to draw on she set out to meet her on the road. Taking Mrs Sheppherd's
account of events, she had walked a good distance towards Mansfield and must
have passed the spot by the side of the road where her daughter's body was later
found. It was around this point that she saw a familiar figure on the road some
distance ahead. Thinking that Bessie had also seen her and would hurry to catch
up, Mrs Sheppherd turned and began to walk home. She was later to recall that
shortly after turning for home she passed a stranger, who was later identified as
Charles Rotherham. She could not have known then that her daughter would
also meet with Rotherham, an encounter that she would not survive.

Charles Rotherham was a 33-year-old ex-soldier from Sheffield. Given the
date it is likely that he was one of those men who had fought in the Napoleonic
Wars. Many had been with the Duke of Wellington for nine years in the
Peninsular Campaign. Some men were volunteers who had joined the army in an

attempt to escape poverty, whilst others had been forced to join as an alternative to penal servitude. At the Battle of Waterloo in 1815, Wellington described the British Army as 'the scum of the earth and the dregs of society'.

With cessation of hostilities, the army was returned to its peace-time levels and thousands of men were discharged back into society by an ungrateful government and left to wonder the country looking for work. Even by 1817 these ex-soldiers were regarded as a problem to decent society. Using whatever skills they had acquired, these men made a living as best they could. Certainly, Rotherham, a married man with children, presented himself as an itinerant 'scissor sharpener'.

Witnesses state that Rotherham had been drinking in the Hutt that afternoon and had left shortly before he was seen by Mrs Shepphard. From the accounts he was heading towards Mansfield. Coming in the opposite direction was young Bessie, happy with the news that she had found work. We do not know if she had seen her mother and had quickened her pace. What we do know is that she met Charles Rotherham at a point on the Mansfield Road where it emerges from the southern side of Harlow Wood.

Rotherham was loitering near the spot where he was to commit the dreadful act. He was later to confess that his attack was completely motiveless and unprovoked. However, an examination of the details given on the handbill published at the time of his execution disputes the fact that the crime was neither spontaneous nor motiveless.

Rotherham's choice of weapon used in the attack suggests a degree of premeditation. Rotherham had pulled up a wooden hedge stake from the side of the road and used it to bludgeon the unfortunate girl about the head and other parts of the body. Such was the violence used, the handbill states, that 'her head presented a most shocking spectacle, being so disfigured that her features could scarcely be recognised; the brains protruded from the skull, and one eye was completely knocked out of the socket, and lay upon her cheek.' As for motive, the handbill indicates that it was robbery when it says, '[he] threw her into a ditch, after taking from her an umbrella, and a pair of shoes; he also attempted to take off her gown, but could not accomplish it'.

Bessie's body was discovered the next morning by a gang of quarrymen on their way to work. One of the men spotted a little trail of half-penny coins which led the way to the gruesome remains. The handbill goes on to say, 'A gentleman and lady, who happened to be riding by in a gig shortly afterwards, and saw the body gave information of the circumstances to the Police Office.' A hue and cry was instantly raised.

After committing the murder, Rotherham, who must have been covered with blood, turn back towards Nottingham. He walked on to Seven Mile House, which at the time was Ginger Beer House. Here he tried to sell the shoes and umbrella, the only proceeds of his crime. It would seem from reports that Rotherham may have been forcibly removed from the premises.

From here, he walked on over Red Hill to the now demolished Three Crowns Inn, which stood opposite The Ram public house. A little aside here; there are references stating that the two public houses were linked by a cave or underground passage.

At the Three Crowns, Rotherham once again tried to sell his ill-gotten gains, but without success. He continued his drinking, even going on to sing a couple of popular song for the price of his ale. Rotherham was to spend the night at the inn. At this time, it was common for those willing to share a bed with others, to take a room at an inn at very little expense. The next morning it would seem that Rotherham may have left in a hurry, for it seems that he left Bessie's shoes in the room. The umbrella he later managed to sell in the village of Bunny.

I have retold Bessie's story many times and the efficiency of the Georgian police force never ceases to amaze me. News of the murder and the hunt for Bessie's killer had been spread as far as Leicestershire. Once again I will let the handbill tell the story:

> From Red Hill he [Rotherham] was traced on the road to Loughborough, and was taken on
> the bridge leading over the canal near that place. He was looking over the bridge into the
> water, when the constable approached him, and accosted him with being his prisoner: he
> made no resistance.

With Charles Rotherham in custody on suspicion of murder, a full Coroner's Inquest was held at the Old Blue Bell Inn in Sutton-in-Ashfield. After the inquest, probably in the face of overwhelming evidence, Rotherham confessed to the murder. He stated that he had no idea why he had committed the crime and that he did not speak throughout the murderous act.

Rotherham was tried for murder in Nottingham and was found guilty on his own confession. He was publicly executed on 28 July 1817 at the gallows on Gallows Hill on Mansfield Road – the same spot as the unfortunate Robert Downes.

Elizabeth Shepphard's remains were given a decent funeral by the outraged populous and interred in Papplewick churchyard. A memorial stone, paid for by public subscription, was erected on the site where her body was found. The main benefactor of this stone was a Mr Anthony Buckles. Was Mr Buckles the gentleman in the gig, mentioned in the handbill?

Over the years, Bessie Shepphard's memorial stone became a familiar landmark on the Mansfield Road. A tradition grew up that the spot was haunted by Bessie's ghost. This was said to appear if the stone was in any way disturbed. There was a period in the 1930s when Bessie's ghost was particularly active. At this time, the old Mansfield Road was being improved to become the modern A60.

Whilst giving a talk on the subject, I was informed by a lady member of the audience that she boarded at a school in Harlow Wood before the war. She was often terrified by tales of Bessie's ghost haunting the grounds of the school, particularly around the time of the anniversary of her death in July.

In the 1950s, a car travelling towards Mansfield collided with the stone. Little damage was inflicted on either the vehicle or the stone. However, the driver reported the incident to the Mansfield Police. Sometime later, a young couple travelling the same route observed a spectral figure hovering over the stone. They were so alarmed by the apparition that they reported it at the same police station.

In 1978, workmen widening the road near the memorial stone claimed to have been terrified by a spectre resembling the dead girl until the job was complete. A particularly strange series of events occurred ten years later. In early June 1988, Bessie's gravestone disappeared from Papplewick churchyard. Immediately there were reports of the appearance of her ghost along the Mansfield Road close to her memorial.

In an attempt to find the missing gravestone, two police officers from Mansfield were interviewed by the media at the site of her memorial. After the interview, one of the officers insisted to his colleague that after touching the memorial, he had had a strange feeling that they should return to the churchyard.

Despite having been a part of the unsuccessful search of the churchyard for the missing stone, the other officer agreed to return to Papplewick. The two policemen walked over the ground which had already been covered by the previous search. On entering the little wood on the edge of the churchyard, the officer who had instigated the new search literally fell over the missing gravestone.

Bessie's gravestone was returned and the grave restored. Hopefully, her spirit is now at rest, at least until the next time either her grave or memorial stone is disturbed.

❧ STONE MAN (THE) ❧

In our hectic lives, we travel the roads of our urban conurbations without a thought for their history. There are probably many readers of this book who are familiar with the busy byways of West Bridgford. At a set of traffic lights, the road from Nottingham divides in two in a large V-shape, becoming the Melton and Loughborough roads. Here, on the broad side of the V, stands a modern block of flats. It is hard to imagine now that this pattern of roads is many hundreds of years old. Travelling from Nottingham and arriving at this junction in the year 1830, what would the scene before us have been like? No buildings, just a large triangular scrubland field and one of the strangest sights in the county. Standing at the point where the roads divide and peering across the field, we would have made out the figure of a one-legged man looking back at us. Strange to us, but to the people of the time he was a familiar sight, having stood there in all weathers for as long as anyone could remember.

So, who was the mysterious figure? He was known as the Stone Man (aka the Nottingham Knight) and the field in which he stood was known as Stone Man Close. If our curiosity had gotten the better of us and like Captain Barker (author of *Walks round Nottingham*) we ventured to take a closer look, we would have found him to be 'a sculptured form of a cross-legged knight miserably mutilated, part of the shield yet remains on the left arm.' Stood before him we would, like Edward Hind in his poem (1835), ask, 'Good mister stone-man, can you tell me who the dickens you were made to represent?' Like Hind, we would not have received an answer. That would take nearly another seventy years. Close examination of the figure would have revealed it to have been that of a fourteenth-century knight in early chainmail armour. Not one-legged, as most people supposed, but with one leg folded behind the other. This indicates that he was never meant to have stood upright in this ungainly pose. These kind of stone figures adorn the tombs of medieval lords and knights in many of our ancient churches. The modelling of the figure is meant to tell us much about the person it represents and the cross-legged style indicates that they were a benefactor to the church. Our question should be how and why did this particular tomb effigy come to be here?

Photographs from a newspaper report of the 1890s show that the Stone Man was not actually alone in the field. He was in fact attached to the largest of a line of stones that ran across the field. These mearstones marked the southern-most boundary of the manor of Nottingham. It would seem that around 100 years earlier, a gang of workmen digging a pond near the boundary unearthed the figure and thought it proper to attach him to the ancient stone. They also took it upon themselves to use another of the stones to bridge a nearby stream. This situation seems to have been accepted by the authorities. We find that the Mickletorn Jury, a group elected by the mayor to annually inspect the boundaries of the city, were appointed to touch the figure or incur a forfeit. And so it was that the Stone Man became part of the landscape and lives of the people of West Bridgeford.

Having stood on boundary duty for several years, experts began to speculate as to who the Stone Man might be. The first suggestion that he was the founder of Flawforth church was soon dropped in favour of the founder of St Giles church, West Bridgeford. However, the style of his armour points to a date of around 1300, which means that we can put a name to the statue. If he was a local knight, then he would have been Sir Robert Luteril, Lord of the Manor around 1315. St Giles was partly remodelled between 1320 and 1350. Robert was probably the man who provided much of the funding and therefore deserved a place of honour in the church. Whoever he was, how did he come to be buried in such a strange place? There is a lot that is questionable about the story of the Stone Man.

In 1893, the field Stone Man Close was purchased by developers Messrs Wright & Hircombe. What became of the mearstones we do not know, but the Stone Man finally came home. The then churchwarden requested that the figure should be removed to the church, and so he was. When the church was remodelled, the arch of the original founder's tomb in the chancel of the old church was re-erected in the new chancel. Curiously, this arch, said to be late fourteenth century, was minus its recumbent statue. Here was placed the Stone Man and here he rests to this day.

⚜ SUMMONING OR DEVIL'S STONE (THE) ⚜

In folklore and tradition there are many ways to summon the Devil. Why anyone should want to do so, I simply cannot image. You might think that the process involves a complicated ritual with potions boiled over a cauldron, but you would be wrong. The simplest way of attracting Old Nick's attention is to walk around in circles. However, this has to be carried out a prescribed number of times in the correct direction – usually 'widdershins', counter-clockwise – at a designated time and place.

Just outside the door of St John's church in the north Nottinghamshire village of Carlton-in-Lindrick, is a large worked stone. Known as the Summoning Stone or Devil's Stone, this was originally part of an ancient font or more likely the base of a cross. Legend states that the stone is resistant to being moved and has been known to fall on those who have tried to put it to other use. More importantly, the legend further states that walking around the stone nine times in an anti-clockwise direction will summon the Devil.

Is the present monument, the old cross base, the real Devil's Stone? A quote from H.H. Henson's book *The Church of England* (1939) may be a reference to the original Devils Stone:

> Over the vestry door at Carlton-in-Lindrick there is preserved a stone which may be a relic of a pre-Christian pagan temple. On it are carved in a semi-circle, the sun, moon and stars, bordered by what may be stalks and heads of wheat or barley, in an allusion to the sun's fertilizing power. A Christian cross has been cut later into the upper rim of the stone which seems to have been adapted at one time to form a tympanum for the head of a Norman doorway.

Henson, who was the Bishop of Durham, implies that the church was built on the site of a pagan temple or prehistoric monument – as were many pre-Reformation churches. Selston church may be another example. It has Nottinghamshire's only confirmed example of a menhir or standing stone on the north side of its churchyard. Certainly, the legend and the stone above the doorway seem to confirm Henson's theory.

Did the original summoning ritual involve walking nine times around the stone above the door, and thus around the whole church? We can imagine that if this was the case, it would take much more effort to circumnavigate the church than it does a single stone. For this reason the ritual and thus the legend may have been transferred to a convenient stone in the churchyard.

So if you want to summon the Devil, go to Carlton-in-Lindrick and walk nine times around the stone by the door. If this doesn't work try exercising your legs further and walk nine times around the church. But beware, the old legends never tell you how to get rid of the Devil once you have summoned him.

The Summoning Stone. (Courtesy of Joe Earp)

$\mathcal{T}$

❧ TRENT (THE RIVER) ❧

At 185 miles (294km) long, the River Trent is one of England's major rivers. For around half of its length, from its source on the slopes of Biddulph Moor in Staffordshire, the Trent flows in a roughly easterly direction. Around Radcliffe-on-Trent it begins to take a more northerly direction and from Newark-on-Trent is flowing almost due north. This part of the river forms a natural boundary between the counties of Nottinghamshire and Lincolnshire. The Trent ends its journey at Trent Falls, where it joins the River Ouse to become the Humber, which finally empties into the North Sea near Grimsby.

The Trent is a tidal river, and in ancient times, using this flow, was navigable beyond Nottingham. Later, human and natural constraints on the river, including the building of Trent Bridge limited navigation and reduced the tidal flow. In the year AD 867 the Danish Vikings came up the Trent to Nottingham and Repton in their longships. A little known fact is that the Trent – like the River Severn – exhibits a 'tidal bore' known as the Trent Aegir. When conditions are right the Aegir produces a 5ft (1.5m) wave which travels inland as far as Gainsborough. Without modern constraints, the Aegir's effect would have been felt as far as Nottingham.

The River Trent, like most rivers and other natural features, derives its name from the earliest recorded language in Britain. It is believed that the name is formed from two Celtic words, *tros* (over) and *hynt* (way) producing *tros-hynt* (over-way). Because of the river's tendency to flood and alter its course, this has been interpreted as meaning 'strong flooding' or more directly 'the trespasser'. Another possible meaning is 'a river that is easily forded'. The name *Trisantona Fuvis* (Trisantona River) for the Trent first appears in *The Annales*, the work of the Roman historian Tacitus. Researchers at the University of Wales suggest the name is derived from the Romano-British (again Celtic) *Trisantano* – 'tri-sent (o)-on-'a (through-path) – which has been given the enigmatic interpretation of 'great feminine thoroughfare'. If this is correct, does it suggest that the river was regarded as a manifestation of a Celtic goddess?

Until comparatively recently, with the acceptance of the concept of the Midlands, the geographical location of the Trent was acknowledged as the

FEE

The author's impression of the Clifton Pile Settlement and Bronze Age life on the River Trent.
Recent aerial photos reveal that there are more prehistoric monuments in the Trent Valley than
in the whole of Wessex. (Author's Illustration)

boundary between northern and southern England. The course of the Trent
and Humber separated the tribal territories of the Coritani to the south and
the Brigantes to the north. The Romans, under the Emperor Claudius, invaded
Britain in the year AD 43. For political and other reasons, the Roman Army
did not cross the Trent into Brigante territory until AD 71. In medieval times,
the Royal Forest was subject to a separate 'Justice in Eyre' on different sides of the
river and the jurisdiction of the Council of the North started at the Trent.

As indicated by one of the interpretations of the name Trent, the idea of a
north-south boundary was not regarded as a physical barrier. Along the course
of the river, there are a surprising number of places with the Celtic *rid* (rhyd),
meaning ford, element in their name, indicating the site of an ancient ford
(for example, Ridware). The Anglo-Saxon element ford in place names like
Wilford – where in 1900 a Roman ford was discovered – demonstrates that
these fords were in use for many generations. These fording places were not
just a place where a track crossed a river. At Wilford, the way across the water
was paved, and black oak piles on either side marked its root. This was probably
typical of such sites. That these ancient fords were later replaced by a bridge is
demonstrated by places like East and West Bridgeford. This does not mean that
there were no bridges in earlier times. There is evidence to show that there
may have been a Roman stone bridge at Barton-Island near Attenborough.

In 1985, the remains of a wooden bridge of distinctly Viking workmanship – dating from the early eleventh century – were discovered in gravel workings around Castle Donnington.

There are many legends about the Trent. An omen of a coming death in the Clifton family was said to be the sight of a Royal Sturgeon, swimming up the Trent and turning around in circles in the waters below the hall. The last sturgeon recorded in the river was an 8ft 6in fish weighing 18 stone, caught at Muskham in 1902. Fifteen years earlier, in 1887, a sturgeon weighing 12 stone 12 pounds had been caught at Stokebardolph.

Another local legend is similar to that of the River Dart in Devon, where an old rhyme says 'River Dart, River Dart. Every year thou claims a heart.' The Trent is said to be dangerous, and must claim four lives a year to make it is safe. Could it be that gruesome finds in the river near Clifton offer an explanation for this old belief?

❧ UMBRELLA (BESSIE SHEPPHERD'S) ❧

Bessie Sheppherd's Umbrella is a curiously shaped thorn tree which stands on the eastern side of the A60 Mansfield Road, by the junction of Rickett Lane. The tree, which, as the name suggests, resembles an umbrella, is said to commemorate Elizabeth 'Bessie' Sheppherd, who was murdered at a spot a less than half a mile north of the tree. The site of the murder in Harlow Wood is now marked by a memorial stone which was erected by public subscription soon after the event. It was a yellow umbrella, stolen from the girl, which helped to convict her murderer, Charles Rotherham. Rotherham still had the umbrella about his person when he was apprehended on a bridge near Loughborough in Leicestershire.

There is no record of the tree having been especially planted and it would have taken many years for a new tree to have achieved this size and shape. If the Umbrella Tree commemorated the murder, why was it not planted closer to the memorial stone and site of the murder? It therefore seems likely that a thorn tree existed on this site long before the murder in 1817. It is easier to imagine that an existing tree (which may already have resembled an umbrella) was adapted and became associated with the unfortunate Bessie Sheppherd, rather than a new tree being planted and shaped.

Individual thorn trees were often planted to mark sacred places, as boundary markers or close by holy springs and wells. Devotion to such trees meant that they were constantly looked after by successive generations, with new trees planted when the originals died.

The location of the Umbrella Tree close to the junction of Mansfield Road and Ricketts Lane is a significant one. Ricketts Lane has strong associations with the nearby Alter or Druid Stone at Blidworth. The lane is said to be an approach or ritual way to the stone.

Thorn trees, particularly hawthorn and blackthorn, have long been regarded as sacred. It is said that the hawthorn has more connections with ancient beliefs and folklore than almost any other tree or shrub. It has particular associations with May Day and the ancient festival of Beltane, and is often referred to as May Blossom. It was also regarded as having supernatural powers and was able to ward-off the 'evil eye' and the curse of witches.

The veneration of the thorn tree continued well into the Christian era with the Cult of the Thorn associated with the Glastonbury Thorn. This tree (a Mediterranean or Middle Eastern species) is said to have grown from the staff of Joseph of Arimathea.

In more modern times the thorn became popular for hedging. When planted in a group or as a hedge, thorns can form an almost impenetrable barrier, but when growing alone often produce a substantial trunk with a globular to canopy. Standing alone on a wide grass verge, the Umbrella Tree is a fine example of the individual and perhaps sacred thorn tree. Looking at old maps, 'The Bilborough Thorns' and the original 'Cuckoo Bush' may have been further Nottinghamshire examples.

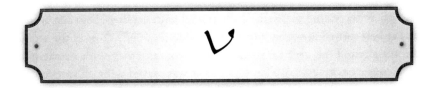

✣ VICTORIAN FOLLY ✣

In 1856, Alderman Thomas Herbert, a wealthy and successful lace manufacturer, built himself a house in Nottingham's fashionable Park Estate. The plot he chose was on a road at the top of a hill to the west of the castle, Victoria Street. Victoria Street was later renamed The Ropewalk and the house is now No. 32 The Rope Walk.

For his gardens, Herbert purchased land overlooking the park. However, this was on the slopes of the hill on the opposite side of the road and in order to gain private access, he had to construct a tunnel. Where the tunnel emerged it was necessary to remove large quantities of sand and soil. As a result, Nottingham

Daniel in the Lion's Den cave. The massive scale of the work can be judged by comparing the carvings with the human viewer. (Courtesy of the Paul Nix Collection)

historian J. Holland Walker (1928) says, 'he found himself in the possession of several caves on the terraces overlooking the Park.'

As well as decorating the walls of the tunnel with carvings, between 1856 and 1872 Herbert turned the caves into what became regarded as one of the wonders of Nottingham. One cave he turned into a conservatory with exotic plants. Of the conservatory cave, Walker says that it was carved with 'all sorts of weird beasties carved in the rock to look as if they were lurking amongst the plants.'

The cave adjoining the conservatory was made to resemble an ancient temple – Walker calls it Egyptian – with rows of pillars and carvings of Druids, sphinxes, gods and goddesses and other strange creatures. Perhaps the most spectacular of the caves is that which opens out onto the garden terrace. The cave mouth is not just a yawning opening, but a complete building façade including pilasters, windows and a door reminiscent of Petra in Jordan. Within the cave are life-size carvings representing the Bible story 'Daniel in the Lion's Den'.

Thomas Herbert was very pleased with his creations, which showed off his wealth and tastes, and for many years he was pleased to put them on public display. 'Daniel in the Lion's Den' became the most celebrated and talked about work of art in Nottingham – but how times and tastes change. By the time Walker published his work *Links with Old Nottingham*, fifty-six years later, the caves and their carvings were no longer in vogue. Walker, in his introduction

Close-up of the standing lion. (Courtesy of the Paul Nix Collection)

to the caves, says, 'So inartistic are these carvings considered nowadays that it is no great loss to the community that they are not accessible to the public, but when they were carved in 1856 they were looked upon as the last word in artistic achievement.'

Not surprisingly over the last eighty or so years, opinions on Herbert's caves and their carvings has changed once more and Geologist Tony Waltham, in a report on conservation of the caves, says, 'Without doubt the finest single feature within the sandstone caves that underlie Nottingham is the group of statues depicting "Daniel in the Lions Den".'

Time, human activity, including deliberate vandalism, and the effects of the direct exposure to the weather outside the cave, has reduced the Daniel statues to a shadow of their former glory. Today, the statues lie behind air-tight doors and shutters fitted to the original openings in 2005 by the East Midlands Geological Society.

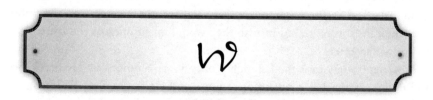

✤ WELL (HOLY): ✤
ST ANN'S OR ROBIN HOOD'S WELL

It is hard to imagine now that the area covered by the St Ann's district of Nottingham was once a part of Sherwood Forest. With a few scattered dwellings, it remained covered in rough pasture and woodland until the mid-1800s. The most important building was the house occupied by the Woodward, an officer of the mayor appointed to manage this part of the forest.

On high days and holidays, the people of Nottingham flocked in their thousands to this spot and had done so for generations. 'Thither do the Towns-men resort by an ancient custom beyond memory.'

It was not just the civic dignitaries and the common folk of Nottingham who visited the Woodward's house. James I and his court, including Lord Gilbert, Earl of Shrewsbury, stopped to refresh themselves on returning from a hunting trip in the forest. They did so by drinking the barrels of the Woodward dry.

What attracted the good folk of the town in such numbers to such a remote place? It was not the Woodward's ale! The answer is the ancient holy well' known officially as 'St. Ann's Well' – called by the people, 'Robin Hood's Well'.

The well is described in 1797 as being under an arched stone roof of rude workmanship. It was noted as being the second coldest in the country – in fact the water being so cold that it would kill a toad. Bathing in the water was believed to cure rheumatic pains and all manner of illnesses.

We must not feel sorry for the Woodward, who received a visit from the king. It seems that successive Woodwards exploited the fame of the well and the house became a money-making victualling house – a café or pub. An eighteenth-century description says that it was surrounded by 'fair summer houses, bowers or arbours covered by plashing and interweaving of oak-boughs for shade.' These were equipped with large oak tables and earth banks for seating. Here the public could dine on food from the kitchen or provide their own food to be cooked on the premises. All this was doubtlessly accompanied by copious amounts of ale purchased from the owner. Two large rooms were provided for the dinners in inclement weather.

Visits to the well were popular throughout the year, with the summer months attracting the most visitors. However, particular attention was made at Christmas, Easter and Whitsuntide.

At a very early date, a little museum dedicated to Robin Hood had been set up. This contained items said to belong to the outlaw. These included his cap – a metal helmet – and his bow. An unusual item was a small ivory tusk said to be Robin's tooth. Central to the exhibition was a large wicker chair, known as Robin Hood's Chair. Young men were charged for the privilege of sitting in the chair and 'saluting' their lady friends and thus being recognised as a member of The Brotherhood of the Chair.

The museum and its contents lasted well into the eighteenth century. However, the chair had received so much attention that it had fallen to pieces and only a small panel was displayed at this time.

An obscure medieval reference speaks of a darker practice about the well. The bodies of unfortunate criminals who were hanged on Gallows Hill were taken to St Ann's and hung in chains from trees about the well.

It is to the early medieval history of the well that we must turn to discover the origins of its attraction and why it became known as Nottingham's great spring. St Ann's Well was not an artificial structure, but a natural spring issuing from a sandstone rock outcrop on the side of St Ann's Valley. The term well, rather than spring, was used to imply that the spring head had been covered or artificially channelled in the remote past.

With grazing animals such as deer using it, a natural clearing in the surrounding woodland developed around the spring. Such water sources attracted the attention of the earliest settlers. Water is a life-giving necessity and a safe, reliable supply such as a spring would have been considered as a gift from the gods.

We do not know how many centuries it was before this forest spring was covered and modified. Something different or special about the water – perhaps it was the intense cold – quickly led to the belief that the spring had healing properties. Some form of management of the site and artificial trough or basin to collect run-off is likely to have been in use long before the first Anglo-Saxons arrived in Nottingham.

The earliest written reference to the well gives the name as 'Brodwell' – possibly derived from the Saxon *brod*, a coming together or to shoot or spout. This name was still in use as late as 1301. An alternative name occurring in written references is Owswell. It has been suggested that the element Ows is a localised Saxon word for the goddess Eostre. However, it seems more likely that it is derived from the Saxon *Ostarmanoth* – Easter Month, April – perhaps denoting the time when the spring flowed at its strongest.

By the time of these early references, the well was already considered as a Christian holy healing spring and was under the care of a hermit who lived close by in a stone cell or hermitage. For a small charge the sick could take a full emersion bath in the healing waters. As the site was in a Royal Forest, the hermit of the well was paid a small fee to watch over the king's deer.

In 1216 an event took place that was to set the well on its course in history. In this year, elders of the town met with King Henry III to ask for a repeal of certain Forest Laws to the benefit of the starving poor. Deer in the forest were culled twice a year and it was decided that the product of the spring cull was to be used for the benefit of the town.

The cull in the area around the well was arranged to take place at the time of the Festival of Easter. It was made compulsory for all the townspeople to attend at the well, for a great feast, followed by the distribution of meat. Thus began the annual pilgrimage to the well on Easter Monday. Starting with a service at St Mary's church, a procession of all the folk of Nottingham led by the mayor, aldermen and clergy walked the mile from the town gates to the well. Here, the sick and lame 'took the cure'.

From the time of the First Crusade until 1312, the site was maintained by the Brotherhood of Lazarus – under the aegis of the Knights Templars – from their headquarters in Burton Lazars near Melton Mowbray Leicestershire. For a small donation to the Knights of St John of Jerusalem, the sick of Nottingham, under the watchful eye of the hermit, continued to partake of the curative bath.

In 1314, the Pope ordered the disbandment of the Templars and seizure of their assets. However, in England, under King Edward II, the Templars fared better and it was some four years later that the king began obeying the Pope's edict.

The well continued as a place of healing, under the care of the Knights of St John who began to adopt Templar sites and practices from around 1320. However, increasingly the site came under the influence of the monks of Lenton Priory, who finally 'seized the great spring of the town'. Much to the annoyance of the local population, the priory dedicated the well to St Ann. In 1409, a chapel of the same dedication was built next to the well, thus sealing the priory's authority over the site.

From the time of its construction, to its demolition after the Civil War, Nottingham Castle was a favourite of royalty. It is likely, then, that many of the monarchs staying at the castle or hunting in the Forest of Sherwood paid a visit to the well at St Ann's. At the very least, such was the importance of the well to the town of Nottingham that they would have been familiar with the site.

It is not the well's association with any member of royalty that made the site popular to the common people. If the stories of Robin Hood are to be believed, it was the trysting place of the outlaw. In the *Geste of Robin Hood*, the site is described as being 'one mile under the lynde' (one mile from the town under the forest) and 'not more than a heap of stones, fit only for a hermit or friar'. This description, along with other elements of the story, fits the well site.

Tarbottom's monument (1860), reputed to have been built on or near the site of the well. (Courtesy of the Paul Nix Collection)

Certainly, the people of Nottingham were convinced of a connection between the well and the outlaw and began to refer to it as 'Robin Hood's Well'. This title probably occurred long before any printed ballads began to circulate in the reign of Henry VII.

When the priory at Lenton seized the well, it was along with Buxton and Malvern – both also dedicated to St Ann – rated as being one of the three great healing wells of England. It is likely that the seizure was motivated out of acquiring a lucrative source of revenue rather than a religious site.

Whatever the motivation, the monks' control of the site lasted until the priory's dissolution in 1536. From this time on, St Ann's Well – as it was now called – was administrated by the mayor and Corporation of Nottingham. Slowly the site became increasingly secular and the chapel began to fall into ruin. Between 1543 and 1534 the records of the Corporation show money paid for repairs to 'Sainte An' Chappel'. By 1577 records show that the chapel had become ruinous and to have been partly absorbed into the Woodward's House.

Although the annual procession to St Ann's had become more of a civic event, it ceased with the outbreak of the Civil War in 1642. Because of this increased secularisation of the site, St Ann's survived the Civil War and Commonwealth. With the Restoration, the well once again became popular.

The Enclosure Act of 1773 saw development of the area. By the early 1800s, the old Woodward's – which had become a public house – become a rowdy out-of-town drinking den. In 1825 matters had become so serious that the pub's licence was revoked and for thirty years it became a tea room, after which a private house.

In 1857, the Corporation Engineer, Mr Tarbottom, realised that future development of the area threatened the site and constructed a large Gothic-style monument over the well. However, things now become a little confused and there is some dispute as to the well's precise location.

In 1887 all buildings in the area were demolished to make way for the long-anticipated Nottingham Suburban Railway and it was believed that the monument and well were covered by one of the supports for the Wells Road Viaduct.

The railway and viaduct were demolished in 1957 and new properties built on the land. In 1987, with the demolition of the Gardeners public house, the site of the well was believed to have been discovered in the pub's car park.

This site was privately excavated by Mr David Greenwood and the results subsequently published.

❧ WISE MEN: ☙
THE WISE MEN OF GOTHAM

'Ha, ha, ha, ha, ha, I must neds laughe in my selfe,
the wise men of Gotum are risen againe.'

Misogonus, 1560

Indeed, the Wise Men of Gotham are 'risen again'. The Gotham Tales are a cycle of stories about feign madness and are closely associated with the village of Gotham in Nottinghamshire.

In the reign of King Henry VIII, around the year 1540, an amusing collection of twenty stories were published under the title of *The Merry Tales of the Mad Men of Gotham* by the mysterious 'A.B. of Phisicke Doctor' (medical doctor). With subsequent editions, the word 'mad' was changed for 'wise' and the myth of the Wise Men of Gotham was born. The pseudonym A.B. was a clever ploy by the publisher of this time to make people believe (successfully it seems) that the author was none other than Andrew Borde. Borde had been the doctor to the king and was a famous travel writer and humourist. Borde never denied or accepted involvement in the publication. Such was the popularity of the work it continued to be re-published almost unchanged to the end of the nineteenth century.

The Gotham Tales were exported to America by Washington Irvine, who then spawned the title of Gotham City (a city of fools) on his native New York. This in turn developed into the Gotham City of *Batman*. The American connection to Gotham does not end there. In the 1995 Presidential election, both candidates, Presidents, George Bush Snr and William (Bill) Clinton, claimed to have ancestral links to the village of Gotham. Clinton, whose birth name is William Jefferson Blythe, claimed decent from the Blythe family of Gotham. However, it was Bush who trumped this by claiming decent from Mary St Andrew, daughter of William St Andrew, Lord of the Manor of Gotham. William's memorial can still be found in Gotham's St Lawrence church.

What are the *Tales of the Wise (Mad) Men of Gotham* all about? There is a universal myth of a town or village inhabited by mad men. This myth originated long ago when few people travelled beyond their own parish boundaries. At this time, most people gained their view of the outside world from those brave souls who dared to venture beyond the parish bounds. News was also brought by travellers passing through, like the local carrier – a sort of long-distance lorry driver – and later by the postman. Human nature dictates that no one really wanted to hear that the ordinary folk in the next town or parish lead the same humdrum life as themselves did, nor did they want to hear that they were somehow better than themselves.

Imagine a carrier arriving in your village and telling you this story:

> I heard tell that there was a man from the village of Gotham who was on his way to market in Nottingham with two bushels of wheat tied about his horse's back. When he got to the top of a hill, the old horse looked almost done in. So, he gets off his horse, takes the wheat from the horse's back and puts it around his own neck. Then, would you believe, he gets back on his horse. "There!" says he, "You were looking tied, so I've taken the burden on myself!" They are all like that in Gotham don't you know.

The tale of the man with the bushels of wheat is not only one of the Gotham Tales but also one of the world's oldest jokes. It is said to have happened in many hundreds of places and not just Gotham. But the good folk of Gotham give a good reason for one of their number committing such a foolish act. In fact, if the legend is true, sometime in the twelfth century, the entire male population of the village were all committing acts of lunacy at the same time. The twenty stories contain an oral tradition that the villagers of Gotham all feigned madness to prevent the wicked King John from coming to their village. In the very act of feigning madness is wisdom and instantly they ceased to be 'mad men' and become 'wise men'.

Although the King John story is the founding tale of the Wise Men of Gotham legend, it has never made an appearance in any of the editions of the twenty tales chap book. The story has, over the many centuries, seldom made an appearance in print, but has remained a tale for the telling. I will tell the story here as Alfred Stapleton might have heard it when he visited Gotham in 1899 whilst researching his book on the Tales.

The people of Gotham were very troubled. They had heard that the wicked King John was planning to visit their village. Someone had said that John was planning to build a hunting lodge in Gotham; another had said that it was to be a castle. Yet another said that the king was merely planning to pass through the village. Whatever the reason for the visit, the Gothamites knew that it would bring disaster and ruin on their village. The building of a hunting lodge or castle would mean the loss of valuable farming land or, even worse, the destruction of the entire village. If it was to be that the king was merely passing through the village they would forever be liable for the upkeep of the road on which he travelled. In those days, whatever road the king travelled along became a King's Highway and the owners of the land over which it passed had to pay for its upkeep, in case the king wished to use it again.

The good people of Gotham gathered together in the church to discuss the imminent arrival of King John. How do you defy a king, especially one like John? Short of taking up arms in open rebellion, which would be punishable by death, what could they do? There was not time to summon the help of the famed outlaw Robin Hood. By the time they had sent a message to Sherwood Forest the king would already be at Gotham.

They needed time to hatch a plan. Three young farmers volunteered to go out on the road and delay the king's arrival. As they set off towards Nottingham, the three young men knew that they were risking their lives. On arriving on Gotham Moor – to the north of the village – they heard the news that the king was without his usual escort of armed men and had already crossed the Trent.

(To briefly interrupt the story. Stapleton found that those who related the story to him insisted that John was travelling in his chariot. Whilst the use of the word chariot is a Victorian slang word for a kind of two-wheeled gentlemen's carriage, I believe that it here indicates that the original story is far older than the reign of King John.)

The three farmers waited on the moor by a mound. They had brought with them a length of iron chain and, along the way, cut a large stake from a nearby wood which they hammered into the centre of the mound. It had been decided that the only way to give their fellows more thinking time was to physically stop the king. It was not long before King John arrived. As his chariot passed the mound, one of the farmers rushed out in front of the horses, forcing the driver to bring the vehicle to a sudden stop. The second man quickly tied one end of the chain around the stake whilst the third man wrapped the other end around the axle of the chariot.

The king was furious; shaking his fist at his attackers he called out, 'I know you are men of Gotham! A pox on your village, I will burn it to the ground and kill every one of you!'

King John's encounter with the three Gotham farmers had left him badly disturbed. With the help of a blacksmith and men from Clifton, he managed – after several hours – to free his chariot from the chain. Returning to Nottingham Castle, at first he was furious with the Gothamites and determined to exact his revenge by sending his men-at-arms to burn down the village. Now, given time to think about things, he had calmed down.

John knew he was not popular, but why would three men be so desperate as to stop the king in his progress? Was it the start of a wider rebellion? John decided that he would not risk sending armed men into a suspected ambush. He would send an envoy to Gotham to investigate.

Meanwhile, the three farmers had returned to Gotham, worried that they had made matters worse. However, their delaying tactics had given the rest of the village time to hatch a cunning plan. They would all pretend to be mad. Everyone knew that madness was contagious and King John would forgive them their actions and would not dare go near the village. Early next morning the Gothamites received word that the king's envoy was on his way to the village.

When the envoy arrived in Gotham, he found the villagers engaged in crazy acts. Some were trying to drown an eel in the village pond, others were building a hedge around a bush, in an attempt to keep in a cuckoo, yet others were rolling cheeses down a hill to find their own way to market. Everywhere he looked he saw madness. Straightaway he turned his horse around and galloped back to his master to report these strange events. When John heard the news, he realised that Gotham was full of 'mad men'. The plan had worked; John never did visit Gotham. It is said that whenever John heard the name Gotham a wry smile creeped over his face. Was this relief at not facing a rebellion or because he was the first to see the joke?

There are said to be over 100 Gotham Tales, far too many to relate here. There is one, however, that is perhaps the most famous: the Cuckoo Bush Tale. Though it has always appeared as tale No. 3 in the chap book, it has played an important role in promoting sales. It has always provided the only illustration in the book, appearing as it does on the front cover of every edition of the Tales ever published.

The story is here given in the words of the 1630 edition of the Tales:

> On a tyme, the men of Gottam would haue pinned in the Cuckoo, whereby shee should sing
> all the yeere, and in the midst of ye town they made a hedge round in compasse, and they
> got a Cuckoo, and had put her into it, and said: Sing here all the yeere, and thou shalt lacke

THE
MERRY TALES
OF
The Mad-Men of *Gotam.*

By *A. B.* Doctor of Phyſick.

Coocou

Gotam

printed by J. R. for G. Coniers, at the Golden-Ring,
on Ludgate-Hill, and J. Deacon, at the Angel in
Guile-Spur-ſtreet without Newgate.

Front cover of 1640 edition of *The Merry Tales*. (Author's Collection) neither meate nor drinke. The Cuckoo, as soone as she perciued her selfe incompassed within the hedge, flew away. 'A vengeance on her!' Said they: We made not our hedge high enough'.

There are over forty villages in England which claim the Cuckoo Bush Tale (and sometimes others of the Gotham cycle) as their own. However, the people of Gotham have proof of their ownership of the tale. On a hill to the south of Gotham stands the Cuckoo Bush Mound, the legendary spot where the wise men attempted to pen in a cuckoo. Reputedly, at the very centre of this mound, until the early 1800s, was to be found the very bush in which the bird perched. So popular an attraction did this site prove to be that Earl Howe – owner of the land – had it cut down and increased the size of the wood which now covers the site.

The mound and the wood in which it stands remain in private hands and there is no public access. The mound is described as probably a tumulus, a prehistoric burial mound, though there is no proof of this. But can there be another explanation for the existence of both the mound and the tale? Folklore associates the cuckoo with the rites of spring. In the distant past, before the birds' migration to and from Africa was understood, it was believed that the cuckoo spent the winter in a fairy mound – tumulus. There are a number of other cuckoo mounds and cuckoo pens throughout the country, particularly on the Berkshire Downs. All purport to be the place where a cuckoo was hedged, fenced, walled or penned in. Could it be that such mounds were purposely built for the cuckoo to spend the winter months in? Is the cuckoo-penning legend a folk memory of an ancient ritual where a live bird was buried in the mound to ensure the return of spring? This author thinks so!

❧ XYLOPHONE MAN (THE), FRANK ROBINSON ❧

'I don't pretend that I'm Mozart,
I'm just having a bit of fun and keeping people entertained.'

Frank Robinson, 2003

Anyone who has ever walked along the busy shopping street of Listergate in Nottingham's city centre, before 2004, would have heard the distinctly unmelodious sound of a 'tinkling' xylophone. This assault to the ears was the music of Frank Robinson, Nottingham's favourite busker.

Frank was certainly no musician, even by his own admission. He was there to entertain and would simply bang out random notes in an attempt to play a tune. Around Christmas time, Frank's music would vaguely resemble popular

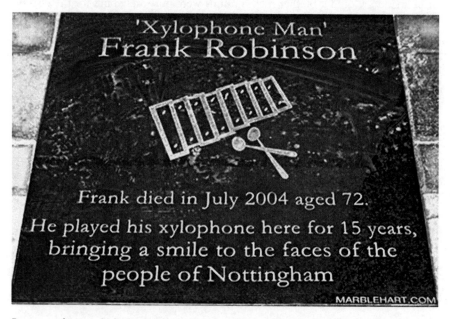

Pavement plaque to 'Xylophone Man' in Listergate, Nottingham. (Courtesy of Joe Earp)

carols. Frank was a very private man and until his death in 2004, few people knew his real name and he was popularly known as 'Xylophone Man'. However, the instrument he used was in fact a child's toy known as a metallophone.

Frank was born in 1932, in the village of Cotgrave some 5 miles south-east of the centre of Nottingham. Nothing is known of his early life – Frank only ever gave one interview – but he continued to live in Cotgrave until his death. Sometime around 1989, Frank took to busking and began his daily commute to the city centre. His favourite pitch was outside the C&A store in Listergate. A small man with white hair and beard, Frank sat on a little wooden stool with his xylophone on his lap. Striking the instrument with rubber-tipped wooden sticks, he would often produce the same three or four notes repeatedly. Frank's pitch was strategically placed and because of its enclosed position, the sound could be heard from one end of the street to the other. It was certainly not the quality of his music that endeared him to the good folk of Nottingham, but rather his child-like enthusiasm and ready smile. In fact, Frank earned himself something of a cult status.

Frank gave his one and only interview to Jared Wilson, from Left Lion media organisation, in June 2003. At the time Frank was 72 years old. Among the few facts that he revealed about himself was that he had used several xylophones over the years and that his current instrument was his favourite. After his death it was discovered that Frank owned twenty-five xylophones, his first having been brought from a charity shop at the start of his career.

Frank Robinson, Xylophone Man, died from a heart attack at the queen's Medical Centre on 4 July 2004 at the age of 73. His funeral, attended by over 100 people including representatives of the city council, took place at the chapel on Wilford Hill in West Bridgford. On 10 November 2005, a memorial plaque was unveiled on the very spot where Xylophone Man sat.

❧ YULETIDE IN SHERWOOD FOREST ❧

When do we begin to celebrate Christmas? In true Christian terms, the festival of Christmas does not begin until the evening of 24 December – Christmas Eve – and lasts for twelve days until 6 January, Epiphany.

The Twelve Days of Christmas were originally part of the great Germanic pagan festival of Yule. The Victorians loved the idea of Yule as part of John Ruskin's idea of Merry England, the revival of the customs and traditions of an idyllic past. Along with ideas introduced from his homeland, Prince Albert's Germanic roots served to encourage the celebration of Yule as an integral part of Christmas.

In 1835, the American writer and diplomat, Washington Irving, published his book *Abbotsford and Newstead Abbey*. The book is a personal account of his stay with his friend Colonel Wildman, at Newstead Abbey in 1824. Wildman, a veteran of Waterloo, had purchased the abbey from Lord Byron in 1817, with money from the family's sugar plantations.

At the time of its publication, Irving had returned to America after living and travelling around Europe for over twenty years. Irving was an accomplished travel writer and Anglophile and produced some of the finest accounts of life in Victorian Britain.

Washington Irving began Christmas 1824 at Barlborough Hall in Derbyshire near Chesterfield – 17 miles from Newstead. At Barlborough and Newstead, Irving states that he witnessed many of the rustic festivals that urban dwellers had declared obsolete: 'I had seen the great Yule log put on the fire on Christmas Eve, and the wassail bowl sent round brimming with its spicy beverage.'

The Yule Log was always brought into the house with great calibration on Christmas Eve. It was chosen as the largest possible hardwood log to fit the hearth. Ignited from the charcoal of its predecessor, it was intended to burn for the full twelve days of celebrations. There is some folkloric evidence to suggest there was an ancient belief that contained within the log was the coming spring. An old Irish folk story, rewritten by the blind Irish poet and writer Frances Browne, tells how a cuckoo emerged from a Yule Log put onto the fire by a poor cobbler.

The word 'wassail' is a contraction of the Middle English *waes haeil* and means 'good health' or 'be you healthy'. It was used as a salute in the form of a toast with hot mulled cider (later hot mulled wine). As well as its association with Christmas/Yule, it was primarily a part of the apple harvest custom. After the fruit was harvested, the trees were saluted with a wassail to ensure future harvests. The apple is a fruit very much associated with the pagan 'otherworld'.

It is likely that Irving participated in another popular seasonal entertainment, the game known as snapdragon or flapdragon. The house lights were dimmed or extinguished and a large, flat bowl filled with brandy and raisins was set alight. The object of the game was to pluck the fruit from the burning mass. The earliest record of the game is from the sixteenth century, although it may be much older. At least one Victorian writer – Chambers in his *Book of Days* – suggests that it is the survival of an ancient winter 'fire festival'.

Bringing in the Yule Log. (*Chamber's Book of Days*)

Irving enjoyed his Christmas/Yule revels at Barlborough Hall, but before the Twelve Days were over, he was to experience again all of the seasonal customs the good rustics of Nottinghamshire could offer, when he journeyed south to Newstead Abbey and what he regarded as the heart of Sherwood Forest.

Irving lists the customs and traditions he witnessed at Newstead, including the Wassail Bowl, the Boar's Head, glee singers and minstrels. As well as those we would normally associate with Christmas, Irving includes things that may be unfamiliar to most modern readers, when he says, 'We had mummers and mimers too, with the story of St George and the Dragon, and other ballads and traditional dialogues, together with the famous old interlude of the Hobby Horse ...'

It seems strange that there would be a performance of a play about St George. However, hero combat plays, where two or more characters fight and one of the combatants is slain and is revived by a quack doctor, was once a popular part of any winter celebration. In Nottinghamshire, there is a variant of the mummers play known as a wooing play, where it is a female character – Dame Jane – that is slain and revived.

The traditional hobby horse would once have been a familiar sight at this time of the year. Examples are recorded as early as 1460. Making an appearance from Martinmas (11 November) to Plough Monday, it was often used to raise funds for the parish church.

Twelfth Night Merry-Making in Farmer Shakeshaft's Barn.

The twelfth night; the ideals of a Victorian Christmas, a Victorian print. (Author's Collection)

The English/Welsh hobby horse is known as a hooden horse. It consists of a horse head – often a horse skull – carried on a pole. The operator is covered by a large cape, traditionally made from a horse-blanket. The horse snaps its jaw and chases among on-looks, sometimes leading them in a spiral dance.

In parts of Lancashire, the hobby horse appears under the name of 'Old Ball', whilst in Wales it is known as the 'Mari Lloyd', the Grey Mare. In Christian mythology the mare is the horse turned out of the stable where Jesus was born and doomed forever to wonder the earth looking for shelter. In Nottinghamshire – around Mansfield – the horse is simply known as 'Owd Oss'.

In 1824, Plough Monday fell on 10 January, and Irving was at the abbey to witness the Plough Monday performance. Walking in the cloister of Newstead, Irving heard the sound of 'rustic music and bursts of merriment' coming from within the building. He was invited by the chamberlain (butler) to join the company. Entering the servants' hall he encountered the local Plough Play performance: 'a set of morris-dancers, gayly dressed up with ribbons and hawks-bells. In this troop we had Robin Hood and Maid Marian, the latter represented by a smooth-faced boy; also Beelzebub, equipped with a broom, and accompanied by his wife Bessy, a termagant old beldame.' With the Plough Monday performance over, so too ended Washington Irving's Christmas/Yule in Sherwood.

⚜ ZOO (PRIVATE), THE VICTORIA HOTEL ⚜

The first railway station at Beeston – which was little more than a cottage – was built to service the Midland Counties Railway in 1839 (opened 4 June 1839). In 1844, this company merged with the Birmingham and Derby Junction Railway to form the Midland Railway. In 1847, a much larger station – the current building – replaced the old station to accommodate the ever increasing passenger numbers.

It is true to say that the expansion of the rail network in Queen Victoria's reign changed the face of the country and produced the modern Britain we see today. Fast, reliable transport meant that goods and passengers were able to accomplish journeys that normally took days in a matter of hours.

The Victoria Hotel. (Courtesy of Joe Earp)

Last orders. Ben the bear finishes his pint on the bar of the Victoria Hotel. (Courtesy of Mrs Malaiki Kayani)

In fact, the railways brought about such a revolution that it was necessary to standardise time throughout the country.

The Victorian zeal for railways and the necessary stations was matched only by the building of new inns, public houses and hotels to accommodate the new mobile population. Apart from the casual visitor, those wishing to explore the new horizons brought by the railway, these hostelries were primarily built for the use of the business classes like the commercial traveller. Just about every town or village with a station has within walking distance its own railway hotel or commercial inn. Beeston is no exception.

The Victoria Hotel was built between 1838 and 1839 on land alongside the railway, just over 100 yards from the station. A licence was granted to Mr John Stothard on 13 September 1839 and the hotel was opened 12 March 1840. John Stothard remained the landlord for twenty years and established a business that is still around today. No longer a hotel, the Victoria is now a successful real ale pub and restaurant.

There the story might have ended, if it were not for the actions of an eccentric landlord in the early 1970s. Free from the modern constrains of keeping exotic animals, he was able to establish a mini zoo in the extensive outbuildings to the rear of the property. Among the collection were several small monkeys, three big cats – a puma, a lion and a leopard – a baboon, and a python, which was kept in the main house. There was also a black bear cub called Ben who frequented the bar and finished half empty beer bottles when time was called. The good folk of Beeston were frequently treated to the sight of Ben being taken for a walk at the end of a rope.

Two of the big cats caused their own problems. On one occasion the landlord caused some alarm when he was bitten by the leopard. Another time the puma bounded into the main bar area and terrified the regulars.

Imagine the horror of waking one morning to find a large baboon staring through your bedroom window. Such was the case for an elderly couple who were neighbours to the Victoria. The animal had escaped and had shinned up the drainpipe and was attempting to gain access through the window.

The zoo was finally forced to close after a fire broke out in the monkey enclosure, killing the animals.

Select Bibliography

❧ BOOKS ❧

Beckett, J.V. (ed.), *A Centenary History of Nottingham* (Manchester: Manchester University Press)

Blackner, J., *A History of Nottingham* (Nottingham, 1815)

Briscoe, P., *Old Nottinghamshire* (London: Hamilton, Adams & Co., 1881)

Brown, C., *Notes About Notts: A Collection of Singular Sayings, Curious Customs, Eccentric Epitaphs, and Interesting Items* (Nottingham: T. Forman & Sons, 1874)

Deering, C., *Nottingham via Vetus et Nova* (Nottingham, 1751)

Earp, F.E., *The Catstones of Catstone Hill*, 1st edition (Nottingham: Cuckoo's Press, 1999)

Greenwood, D., *Robin of St Ann's Well Road: Origins of Robin Hood* (Nottingham: David Greenwood, 2007)

Mellors, R., *In and About Nottinghamshire* (Nottingham: J. & H. Bell Ltd, 1908)

Nix, P.A., *A Nottingham Hidden History Team Monograph No. 2, Nottingham Caves: The Ropewalk* (Nottingham: APRA Press, 1988)

Stapleton, A., *All About the Mad Tales of Gotham* (Nottingham: RN Pearson, 1900)

Stukeley, W., *Itinerarium Curiosum Vol. I* (London, 1776)

Walker, J., *An Itinerary of Nottingham, Transactions of the Thoroton Society Vol. XXXII* (1928)

❧ PERIODICALS ❧

Earp, F.E., The Old Stones of Nottinghamshire (at the Edge: No. 6, 1991)

❧ WEBSITES ❧

nottinghamhiddenhistoryteam.wordpress.com [Accessed August–October 2013]

Also from The History Press

Ever Wondered What your Town Used to Look Like?

Our *Then & Now* series sets out to illustrate the changing face of the UK's towns and cities in full colour. Contrasting a selection of forty-five archive photographs alongside forty-five modern photographs taken from the same location today, these unique books will compliment every local historian's bookshelf as well as making ideal gifts for everyone interested in knowing more about their hometown.

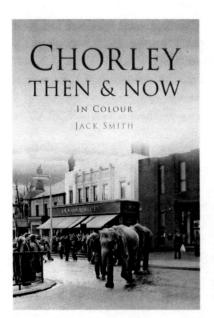

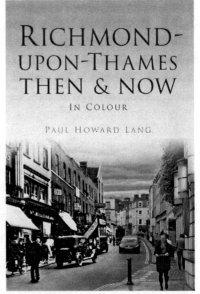

Find these titles and more at
www.thehistorypress.co.uk

Also from The History Press

We are proud to present our history crime fiction imprint,
The Mystery Press, featuring a dynamic and growing list of
titles written by diverse and respected authors, united by
the distinctiveness and excellence of their writing. From a
collection of thrilling tales by the CWA Short Story Dagger
award-winning Murder Squad, to a Victorian lady detective
determined to solve some sinister cases of murder in London,
these books will appeal to serious crime fiction enthusiasts
as well as those who simply fancy a rousing read.

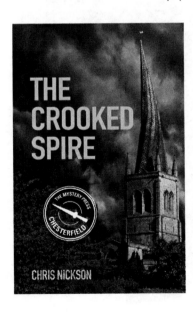

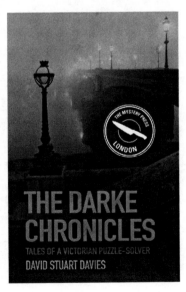

Find these titles and more at
www.thehistorypress.co.uk

Also from The History Press

BACK TO SCHOOL

Find these titles and more at
www.thehistorypress.co.uk

Also from The History Press

WHEN DISASTER STRIKES

Find these titles and more at
www.thehistorypress.co.uk

Lightning Source UK Ltd.
Milton Keynes UK
UKOW05f1511110414

229835UK00002B/37/P